1395

Three Eyes on the Past

Three Eyes on the Past

EXPLORING NEW YORK FOLK LIFE

LOUIS C. JONES

SYRACUSE UNIVERSITY PRESS 1982

This book is published with the assistance of a grant
from the John Ben Snow Foundation.

Library of Congress Cataloging in Publication Data

Jones, Louis Clark, 1908–
    Three eyes on the past: Exploring New York folk life.
    (A York State book)
    Bibliography: p.
    1. New York (State) — Social life and customs —
Addresses, essays, lectures. 2. Folklore-New York
(State) — Addresses, essays, lectures. 3. Folk
art — United States — Addresses, essays, lectures.
I. Title.
F119.5.J66 1982   306'.09747   82-7334
ISBN 0-8156-0179-4 (pbk.)   AACR2

"Foreword to *A Short History of New York State*" from *A Short History of New York State*, by David M. Ellis, James A. Frost, Harold Syrett, and Harry J. Carman, pp. vii–x. Copyright © 1957 by Cornell University. Used by permission of the publisher, Cornell University Press.

"Land of the Upper Hudson" is reprinted with permission from *The Magazine Antiques* (July 1951).

"A Look at Historic Preservation" is reprinted with permission from *The Magazine Antiques* (July 1956).

"Three Eyes on the Past" is reprinted with permission from *New York Folklore Quarterly* (Spring and Summer 1956).

"The Ghosts of New York: An Analytical Study" is reprinted with permission from *Journal of American Folklore* (October 1944).

"The Devil in York State" is reprinted with permission from *New York Folklore Quarterly* (Spring 1952).

"Italian Werewolves" is reprinted with permission from *New York Folklore Quarterly* (Fall 1950).

"Practitioners of Folk Medicine" is reprinted with permission from *Bulletin of the History of Medicine* 23, no. 5 (September-October 1949) (Baltimore, Md.: Johns Hopkins University Press).

"The Berlin Murder Case" is reprinted with permission from *New York History* (April 1936).

"Crazy Bill Had a Down Look" © 1955 by American Heritage Publishing Co., Inc. Reprinted by permission from *American Heritage* (August/September 1955).

"The Triumph of American Folk Art" is reprinted with permission from *Search* 8 (Fall 1978).

"Genre in American Folk Art" is reprinted with permission from John C. Milley, ed., *Papers on American Art* (Philadelphia, Pa.: The Friends of Independence National Historic Park, 1976).

"Outward Signs of Inner Beliefs: Symbols of American Patriotism" is reprinted with permission from The New York State Historical Association (1976).

For Aggie

Louis C. Jones is Director Emeritus of the New York State Historical Association and The Farmers' Museum in Cooperstown. He was graduated from Hamilton College and received the A.M. and Ph.D. from Columbia. A cofounder of the New York Folklore Society and first editor of its *Quarterly*, Dr. Jones is the author of several books, including *Clubs of the Georgian Rakes*, *Spooks of the Valley*, and *Things That Go Bump in the Night*. He edited *Growing Up in the Cooper Country* and has published numerous articles on American folklore and folk art and the roles of museums and historical societies.

Contents

Preface

THE years immediately following World War II were full of yeast for American museums. A new generation entered the field, many of whom came from other types of experience, other disciplines. I was one of those, and in part this volume is a record of the growth that took place in my thinking over the decades that followed. I started to write *change* rather than *growth*, but actually I never ceased to be a teacher, like my grandmother, my father, my wife, my sister, my sons and daughter, two of my nephews, and several of my great-nieces and nephews. I brought to the museum profession an interest in oral tradition, in folklore; my experience at the New York State Historical Association (NYSHA, hereafter) and The Farmers' Museum opened my eyes to much larger aspects of our traditional culture, especially to American folk art.

Over the last thirty-five years tremendous changes have taken place in our concepts of what is the appropriate concern of historians, museums, folklorists. The pages that follow reflect those changes and, I hope, give some sense of the fun I had being part of the scene.

There are some acknowledgments to be made: to James Taylor Dunn for permission to reprint our piece on William Freeman; to Simon Bronner for suggestions on inclusions; to all the students (now parents and grandparents) who collected the mate-

rials in the folklore section and to their informants, few of
whom are still alive; to my son David for some stern advice
which I followed; to all those editors who gave permission to
reprint articles which first appeared in their journals; to Minor
Wine Thomas, Director, for permission to use photographs of
so many objects owned by NYSHA. Last, but most especially, to
my wife, Agnes Halsey Jones, who has shared so many of my interests and corrected for the better so many of my pages over
the years. And laughed at the right times.

Cooperstown   LCJ
Spring 1982

A Point of View

I T was a summer day in the late 1930s. The place was Schoharie, a village dating back to the early eighteenth century,
standing at the northern end of one of New York's most
beautiful, most fertile valleys. The audience of fifty or so were
all my father's age or older, and I was already in my thirties.
Good, gentle people whose ancestors had settled there two centuries before, they had come together for the annual meeting of
the historical society to see old friends and, incidentally, to hear
what the professor had to say.

My message was simple enough but one seldom heard in
such organizations forty years ago. I spoke in praise of the oral
traditions of this area, the legends, ghostlore and witchcraft,
beliefs and customs, songs and remedies of the farm people
back in the valleys and the hunters and woodsmen in the cloves.
At considerable length I discussed Emelyn Gardner's excellent
Folklore of the Schoharie Hills, a pioneering volume published
in 1937 but the field work for which had been done from 1912
to 1918.

I talked the forty-five minutes usual for those occasions
and sat down, rather pleased with myself and completely un-
prepared for what followed. The ancient and honorable president rose, and as he passed me to the podium I was aware that
his face was scarlet. There, in a voice trembling with anger, he
told the society what he thought of me, folklore, and Emelyn
Gardner. History is the story of brave men who fought for their

country and the noble women who bore them, history is concerned with the leaders of men, with the hard-working, honorable yeomen and their merchant cousins and the governments they create. It had been an insult to this society, whose members were descended from the courageous men and women who had cleared this land, to regale them with the superstitions of the county riff-raff, the songs of drunkards, and the lies of lazy oafs who had never done an honest day's work in their lives. Let not such trash as this so much as touch the sacred hem of Clio's garment. I have not recaptured the Ciceronian cadences with which this message had been delivered, but I still hear the echoes; I still relive the feelings of the moment — chagrin, amazement, anger, amusement.

Looking back, I think I understand some of the factors in his reaction. Certainly in part there was the feeling that local history is the province of the successful descendants of the first settlers. Then there was the Victorian belief that anything that wasn't "nice," anything vulgar was to be left unsaid. Another factor is that after Longfellow's *Hiawatha*, local newspaper writers created what soon passed for local legends: Indian maidens' leaps, the ghostly cries of widowed squaws, and a plethora of other stories that floated freely across the landscape. As more serious local historians got to work they saw this kind of tale as unhistory, they called it folklore and tagged it "taboo."

Actually by the 1930s the academic historians — or many of them — were accepting the concept of social history and the work of men like Dixon Ryan Fox and John Krout. The role of the genuine folklorist in collecting the traditional aspects of the culture, carried by word of mouth from generation to generation, was merely an extension of that of the social historian. But the conservative local societies felt safer with earlier definitions of history.

My own approach to folklore had come by way of my interest in literature. One evening fifty-odd years ago, there came to Hamilton College, where I was an undergraduate, Carl Sandburg. In those days Mr. Sandburg was going around the country doing several things: he was working on his great six-volume life of Lincoln; he was still writing poetry; and he was enjoying the prestige that resulted from his recently completed *The American Songbag*, the first great collection of American folk songs. I remember the evening very well. I was a pale imitator of Sandburg's poetry in those days, and I had hoped to hear a good deal of and about his poetry; instead he divided his lecture in three parts: one part on his poetry, one part on Lincoln, and for the third, he got out his guitar and sang American folk songs, the like of which I had never heard. Carl Sandburg was singing songs that had been in the oral tradition in this country for some generations. I cannot say I was very much impressed that night and yet, a few months later, in a New York book store I ran across *The American Songbag* and bought it, a purchase that changed the direction of my life.

I had long been interested in the English and Scotch ballads as I found them in literature courses, and here were many of those same songs still sung in this country; then I found that there were other songs with similar themes, long since composed here and alive in the oral tradition. This was the beginning; from *The American Songbag* I began to read other books of folk songs and then other types of folklore. I discovered that there was a whole body of song and story, legend and custom and, particularly, beliefs that had survived in this country, as it had survived earlier in Europe, from the telling of mothers to daughters, father to sons; much of this found its way into popular print, and this had encouraged the telling.

There are all kinds of snobberies, and I took a quiet pride in the fact that generation after generation of my father's family had been independent farmers as far back as the records went. The farm where my father grew up, close by the Salmon River in Oswego County, had been cleared by his grandfather who left Connecticut at the end of the eighteenth century. We were by heritage upstate New York farm folk, although this came to me second hand from my father who had left the farm as a boy. He took an amused tolerance for my interest in folklore, and the only folk song he could remember from his boyhood was "The Darby Ram," especially the more ribald stanzas. But when it came to gardening, he was full of the oral traditions relating to planting and harvesting; while he did not follow them, he had a kind of patient respect for them. In the late thirties and the forties I was living on a farm in Rensselaer

County, and soon I realized that oral traditions — call it folklore
if you wish — were something that many of my neighbors talked
and often were guided by, slipping them on and off like an old
shoe.

Another book of American folk song I picked up about
1934 was Helen Hartness Flanders' recently published *Vermont
Folk Songs and Ballads*. One of these was a murder ballad,
Henry Green, about a young man who in 1845 poisoned his
bride of less than a week in the village of Berlin, New York.
Here was an opportunity to see the relationship between historic fact and the facts as sung. It also became an opportunity
to study the printed broadside and compare it with the oral tradition. The State Law Library had a considerable body of material about the trial, and I became fascinated with the amount
of social history, folkways, and customs a well-documented
murder trial could present. This one provided me with a picture of the roles of women in a small, mid-nineteenth-century
village, the uses of arsenic, the influence of wealth, the ways of
the arsonist, and it introduced me to crust-coffee. In 1936 *New
York History*, the quarterly of the New York State Historical Association, published my first major article, "The Berlin Murder
Case." Two articles of folklore appeared in that issue, a very
early break in the more conservative tradition of historical societies. It was my first personal contact with an organization that
was to preoccupy a good many years of my life. It also was the
beginning of a life-long fascination with murders — especially
those of earlier times.

On July 4, 1934, the day my eldest son was born, I went to
teach at the New York State College for Teachers, now the State
University of New York at Albany. It was, in those days, a stim-
ulating place to be. I had once asked a professor at Columbia if
he thought teaching experience at Albany would be a handicap
in getting into university teaching; I knew well his violent prej-
udice against Teachers College, Columbia. "No," he said, "it's
the only teachers' college with academic respectability. And everyone knows it." Not everyone did know it, but we tried to tell
them.

The president was a Pennsylvania Dutchman named
Abram R. Brubacher, a classicist, a Yale Ph.D., who had wan-

dered into public school administration, having been superin-
tendent of schools in Schenectady before he became president.
He believed that a teachers' college should educate its students
in the same manner as the best of the liberal arts colleges did. In
addition, give them an awareness of the skills of teaching and
some controlled experience. But first and foremost, give them
breadth and depth of learning. To achieve this he sought
teachers who were creative, who were scholars, but scholars
who could communicate.

Another advantage the college had was its students. They
had everything but money. Because of its high standards we
could pick and choose brilliant young people from all over New
York State, from every racial and cultural background — and
we did. There were descendants of families who had lived in
the same eighteenth-century houses for two centuries, and
there were refugees from Hitler; by and large they came from
unsophisticated backgrounds, and a great majority were within
two generations of a vigorous oral culture.

My interest in folklore was greatly quickened by the presence on the faculty of a man I had met once but whom I had
been hearing about for years. When I was a boy growing up in
Albany, the name of Professor Harold W. Thompson was one
around which there was an ever increasing aura. My father
considered Thompson's one of the most distinguished minds he
knew, so that long before I had sorted him out from my father's
world, he was a symbol for the scholar and gentleman. Ultimately I found him, also, a judge of good whiskey. I recall with
great clarity the excitement in our household when the first
Guggenheim Fellows were announced and, lo! in our papers,
Professor Thompson's name led all the rest. In my father's view
this gave the Guggenheim Foundation a standing and infalli-
bility it never lost.

When I went to Hamilton College that same fall, the legend grew and took on perspective, and when *A Scottish Man of
Feeling* was published, it was considered, as well it should have
been, an accomplishment in which the college could take great
pride. The book was reviewed in the Sunday *New York Times*
during one of my vacations, and my father, who was not above
putting his boy on the path of opportunity, suggested that I take

our copy of the review around to the professor's house, two blocks away.

Some young people are stagestruck; I was "penstruck," and in my eyes to be the author of a book rating a full page in the *New York Times Book Review* was to have reached the brow of Olympus. I suppose I assumed he would grab it from my hand and read every lovely word. He did not. He sat me down and persuaded me (ah, how easy a task!) to talk about myself and Hamilton and the Emerson Literary Society, to which we both belonged. He asked questions and led me on for an hour. Only on the way home, treading the clouds beneath my feet, did I realize that he had never so much as opened up the review I had brought him.

Those twenty-five years in Albany, from 1915 to 1940, were, for Harold Thompson, years in which he drove himself to more and more creativity. First and foremost he was one of the masters in the great art of teaching. His teaching had wit, form, content, but especially it stirred the power to understand and enjoy literature; it aroused the curiosity. Most men would have been satisfied with this. Not he. For years he was the leading organist and choirmaster at the First Presbyterian Church in Albany, and contributing editor of *The Diapason*, the organists' magazine. Music was of great importance to him; he insisted on students' singing Shakespeare's songs in his Shakespeare course and, later, folk songs in his folklore classes. He saw music and literature as sister arts: to teach one was to teach the other.

It was in this climate that Thompson began offering his course in American folklore in 1934. So far as I can discover, this was the first time a course covering a large segment of our folk culture was offered to undergraduates, and it became the model for many to follow in later years. There was, of course, no textbook, but with President Brubacher's cooperation and Thompson's guidance, the library soon built up a very good collection of books in the field.

It was inevitable that he put great emphasis on folk song. He had studied the ballad under George Lyman Kittredge, as did so many of the pioneers in our field; his classes *sang* songs, they did not read them. Scornful of education courses, he took immense pleasure in knowing how disturbing it was to courses in educational psychology or tests and measurements to hear "What Shall We Do with a Drunken Sailor?" bellowed forth by a hundred lusty voices from 2 to 2:50, Monday, Wednesday, Friday.

One of the ironies and one of the great innovations of his course in American folklore was that he insisted that his students go into their own families and their own communities and collect the oral tradition that was there. The irony, of course, was that this was progressive education at its best. The personal and emotional impact on many of these students was tremendous. For one thing, they came to know their grandparents and, in many instances, to gain a whole new respect for their own people and the traditions they represented. He encouraged them to think of folklore in America rather than American folklore; thus the student of middle or southern European background sought to discover what traditions his people had brought here and to learn that these traditions had come to him from another land but were indeed universal.

The psychological values of this course, as it was taught in Albany, can never be measured, but I have some inkling of its impact, because when Professor Thompson went to Cornell in 1940, I was permitted to approximate his course under the same title. Students indeed found a new respect for their country and mankind because they saw themselves as part and parcel of an ancient tradition.

The papers of his students and mine created a huge cross section of tales, songs, local legends, beliefs, proverbs, recipes. Those were the days before tape recorders, and so rarely do we get the exact words of the informant, but we get very close approximations. Today the reports of those students — literally thousands of them — occupy twenty-five filing drawers at the library of the New York State Historical Association in Cooperstown. From his material Thompson wrote his classic book of New York State folklore, *Body, Boots & Britches*, and from the findings of my students I wrote two books of ghostlore, one for children, *Spooks of the Valley*, and one for adults, *Things That Go Bump in the Night*.

I had become especially interested in the folklore of the

supernatural: ghostlore, witchcraft, the evil eye, and a wide range of beliefs. I went into the field myself, and among the old German families in the mountains near Taborton, east of Troy, I found witchcraft beliefs very much alive and magic remedies for ailing farm animals as old as the *Seven Books of Moses*. I talked to women acknowledged to have dark powers; one of them had broken up her son's engagement to a girl of whom she disapproved by causing the girl to break out with crescent-shaped hives. I was told of witch covens that still met in those hills; that was why an A-drag was drawn to a certain crossroad Friday nights and left there upside down so that witches could not meet. I wasn't sure what an A-drag was but recognized a countercharm when I heard about it. Years later looking back on those visits to Taborton, I was shocked to realize how little I had let myself learn. Intent on one kind of folklore, I had closed my eyes and mind to any other facet of the culture. Often I have wondered whether there were fraktur on the walls or carefully decorated chests or chairs. I did not take in the furnishings, or the arrangements of farm buildings; I did not look to see what quilts were on the beds. I found what I was looking for, but blinders were on my eyes. My ultimate concept of folk culture was some years down the road.

To go back to Thompson's *Body, Boots & Britches*: the book was designed for the general reader; it was not designed for the little handful of folklore specialists scattered across the land. The public he had in mind was composed of readers of average intelligence, and he sought to give them some sense of the depth and breadth of the oral tradition of New York. To understand the folklore movement in New York State one must note the public Thompson sought to reach, because if the school of folklorists in New York had one quality in common it was the desire to return to the people themselves an awareness of their own traditions. In general we cared remarkably little what the rest of the folklore fraternity thought about this, and some of them were shocked, as though we were giving away to the great unwashed the secret password of the lodge. We always figured that folklore had come from the great unwashed and that it ought to be returned to them; like money and manure it needed to be spread around.

The decade from 1931 to 1940 was, of course, the period during which America suddenly became aware of the fact that it had a folk tradition. President and Mrs. Roosevelt, the Federal Writers' Project, the Index of American Design, the Federal Arts Project, and scores of other New Deal forces brought to the attention of a confused and struggling people an awareness of their native culture.

In New York State a group of writers began to utilize this material. Carl Carmer had devised a new kind of book with *Stars Fell on Alabama* in 1933, and in 1936 he applied this formula to his native New York with *Listen for a Lonesome Drum* and later with *Dark Trees to the Wind* and *The Hudson* and *The Susquehanna*. Carmer was creating books of folk history, concerned with events as people remembered them; with the happy genius of the poet, he told of Indians, the Cardiff Giant, the Loomis Gang, and of the off-beat religions that grew up along the central east-west pathway of the state. At Cornell University Alexander Drummond wrote and encouraged others to write plays, using folk history and legendry to produce a whole series of dramas for production by granges, local drama societies, and historical groups. His own two plays, *The Lake Guns of Seneca and Cayuga* and *The Cardiff Giant* (with Robert Gard), were delightful stagings of the folklore of the Finger Lakes region. In Worcester, New York, a young clergyman named Wheaton Webb was turning out a weekly column on the folklore of his area in the *Worcester Times*, and down in New Paltz, Warren Sherwood wrote in verse of the uncanny critters and strange doings of the Pang Yang. It was in this atmosphere that Thompson and I began to discuss the possibility of a folklore society in New York State as early as 1938. Both Thompson and I were becoming increasingly region conscious and aware of the limitless possibilities in our own state for folklore exploration and publication. In the late thirties he was preoccupied with *Body, Boots & Britches* and I with my dissertation. By the time these were finished the war was on us, and the distance between Ithaca and Albany was greatly lengthened by the dearth of gasoline, but through our correspondence there is a constant echoing of this project.

In the meantime, other events were taking place which

were to facilitate greatly the creation of a state folklore society. In 1931 Dixon Ryan Fox, who had recently become president of Union College, was elected president of the New York State Historical Association. This brilliant and urbane scholar brought to the Association an awareness of social history, in contrast to the military and political history which had been its principal focus of interest. I do not suppose he was greatly interested in folklore as such, but he saw it as a facet of cultural history, and as early as 1936 *New York History*, the Association's quarterly, had published the articles on New York State folklore mentioned above. In 1938 *New York History* published a general survey of folklore in New York State by Professor Thompson which he had read at the annual meeting held the fall before.

In 1939 the Historical Association moved to Cooperstown from Ticonderoga and shortly thereafter began the collection of rural artifacts which would ultimately grow into The Farmers' Museum. Mr. Stephen C. Clark, Sr. had become interested in the Association, and with his encouragement, with the energetic drive of Dixon Ryan Fox, with the able direction of Edward P. Alexander and then Clifford L. Lord, it was leaping forward in its new concept of the interpretation of the state's history.

The summer of 1944 was the period during which plans for establishing of the folklore society, and its magazine suddenly burst into flower. Thompson was in Ithaca and in poor health but working very hard. For the first time in many years I wasn't teaching summer school but was having a highly productive time at my typewriter. At Thompson's suggestion, early in the summer I went up to Schenectady and talked to President Fox about the possibility of developing a folklore society under the aegis of the New York State Historical Association. I remember that occasion with considerable pleasure. This was, I am quite sure, a new idea to Dr. Fox, but he caught it on the run and headed pell-mell for the goal posts. Before I left his office the whole thing was settled. *Certainly* the New York Folklore Society should appear under the aegis of the New York State Historical Association. There should be a session at the forthcoming annual meeting of the latter organization at which folklore would be stressed. I had gone to Schenectady with hat in hand; I came away with the world in my pocket.

On October 6, 1944, the New York Folklore Society was organized at a meeting of the Historical Association in Albany. That afternoon a group of us active in the new society read papers. Shortly thereafter President Edmund Ezra Day of Cornell assured us a five-year grant to underwrite *New York Folklore Quarterly*, today in its thirty-eighth year.

I suppose every life has watershed years, certainly 1946 was for me. The Guggenheim Foundation awarded me a Fellowship, and I took my family to St. Croix in the Virgin Islands to write a book on the folklore of the supernatural in New York State. Before leaving, I went in to pay a courtesy call on Henry Allen Moe, secretary-general of the foundation. About the time I arrived in the islands things began to happen in Cooperstown where Stephen C. Clark, Sr. had agreed to become chairman of the board of the Historical Association. His first responsibility was to find a new director who would lead both the Association and the newborn Farmers' Museum. He turned for suggestions to his friend Henry Allen Moe who offered him what seems to me in retrospect a most improbable candidate: a professor of English and American literature, with one semester of American history in high school and none since, no administrative experience, one who knew absolutely nothing about museums.

In any event I flew up to Cooperstown and had a long talk with Mr. Clark, becoming infected by his dream for the village and the role the Association would play in that dream. He wanted Cooperstown to become an intellectual and cultural center, balancing the more popular appeal of the Baseball Hall of Fame. He already had plans for what became the Seminars on American Culture. In that first meeting and always thereafter, he was open to suggestions that would enhance the educational role of the Association. He pointed to the already successful junior program as an example of one of many facets he hoped to see multiplied. He could be very persuasive, and he persuaded me. Mr. Clark was a bonafide aristocrat, always putting his emphasis on quality, his confidence in integrity. I served happily under his leadership until his death in 1960, learning from him constantly. Heir to a great fortune, one of the distinguished art collectors of his generation, chairman of the Singer Manufacturing Company, one of the founders of the Museum of Modern Art, he was a dedicated son of Cooperstown, the future of which was of profound concern to him. Looking back over those years, my greatest pleasure derives from my association with him — a wise, generous, highly experienced, highly practical visionary. He seemed to me unafraid, especially of experimentation; one would come up with a suggestion, and he would think it over, asking the right questions, finally he would close the discussion with, "I think it's a sound idea, but how are we going to find out if we don't try it." So we tried it. If it worked, that was fine, it if didn't, there were no recriminations, no blame.

To move from the classroom which I had always greatly enjoyed, to the directing of two museums in the spring of 1947, was an exciting if often puzzling change. Not only was I busy learning about museums but also about the art of administration. As the summer wore on I was increasingly aware of how much I had to learn about museums. I couldn't formulate a working philosophy, yet I had the responsibility for an art museum (Fenimore House) and a folk museum (The Farmers' Museum). One solution was to do some visiting and talk to other directors. My wife, Billie, and I went south, seeing some of the great museums: Winterthur, with what then seemed to me an immaculate frigidity; Williamsburg, where all kinds of fresh techniques were being tried by my friend and predecessor, Edward P. Alexander; Walters Gallery and Monticello and the Smithsonian. These and some others were highly professional, and I learned a great deal.

Then we visited two others, Landis Valley and the Mercer Museum of the Doylestown Historical Society, both very different institutions then than they are today. They had fabulous collections in total disorder. The Landis brothers were packrats with a barn and a house full of great piles of tools, implements, furniture, guns, ceramics, and about forty cats who produced a unique museum aroma. The Mercer collection was housed in the first large poured concrete building in America with hundreds of thousands of items piled high in cubicles protected by chicken wire. After Winterthur, this was the other end of the spectrum. That night in Doylestown I went to bed puzzled and disturbed. I dreamed of a very distinguished scholar under whom I had studied at Columbia. He had an extraordinary number of facts at his finger tips, but he was totally incapable of organizing them into a coherent, useful lecture. Unconsciously I had discovered the profound difference between a collection and a museum; the role of the museum professional is to select from the collection objects which can be put into a meaningful relationship. In short, good museum practice was merely good teaching; a museum was to be thought of as an educational institution. Sixteen years of teaching perhaps were a better preparation for museum work than I had thought. I went back to Cooperstown with a new sense of direction and a new confidence.

It was that same fall that I learned another lesson. George Campbell was the assistant curator at The Farmers' Museum, and he had gone out into the byways of Otsego County with a pick-up truck and single-handedly had collected a large portion of the tools and implements in the museum. He was the ideal field collector. He was farm raised and had had his own farm; he knew personally most of the farmers in the area; he took his time and would chew the fat about any number of subjects before he got around to asking what old things were up in the loft or stored in the carriage shed. I might add parenthetically that George was one of the best tall tale tellers I have ever known and one of God's true gentlemen besides.

One afternoon we were walking around the collection of farm tools, and he was teaching me things I ought to know but didn't. We came to a large triangle made of two-by-fours with great spikes protruding from the bottom. I asked what that was called, and in a voice that implied that any darn fool would know that, he said, "Why, that's an A-drag."

An A-drag. Where had I heard that before? Then I remembered the old lady on Taborton Mountain and the way they had kept the witches from meeting at the crossroad. Maybe Henry Moe had been right: a man who had been concerned with the tales people tell, the songs they sing might have a useful background for working in a folk museum concerned with the tools and the traditional hand skills of rural life.

I began to see our traditional culture as a whole. Not only had songs and tales, legends, and beliefs been handed down from generation to generation but so too had agricultural and craft techniques, hand skills of hearth and loom, patterns of domestic architecture, and many another aspect of our culture. This provided a philosophic base for The Farmers' Museum, because that institution was dedicated to telling the story of rural life in our part of the world between the Revolution and the Civil War, the period that marked the beginning of the end of so many traditional folkways and the rising importance of the printed page on the farm.

Soon I was putting my mind on the role of history and the historical society. Not having been trained as an academic historian but in the field of literature and literary history, and having become deeply interested in oral tradition, my conclusions were somewhat idiosyncratic. The emphasis on wars, politics, and leaders seemed to me overbalanced; I found comfort among the social historians, but I felt one could and should go much further. As for historical societies and their museums, in those days the emphasis was almost universally on the leaders and the rich, and the artifacts were chosen on grounds of association, real or imagined, with them. But it was not enough to look at the icing; it was time to examine the cake itself, to see how the people lived who fought the wars, elected the leaders, and worked for the rich, what they wore and ate, what they believed, what tools they used, and what songs they sang. History had to seek an all inclusiveness it lacked in those days, and a historical society like ours should be free to explore and utilize a wide variety of disciplines concerned with the past and its relation to the present.

This approach found expression in the Seminars on American Culture which we began to offer in July 1948. As I have already indicated, Stephen C. Clark, Sr. (and his friend Carlton J. H. Hayes, who was soon to become president of the association) had had in mind some sort of summer adult education program to be developed by the new director when he arrived on the scene. Parenthetically, this was characteristic of Mr. Clark who believed that the role of trustees was to set policy and to leave to the staff the implementation with no interfer-

ence. If more trustees really understood this simple arrangement, there would be fewer tragedies among the arts organizations of the country. What we decided to do was to base the
courses to be offered on the areas where we had considerable
strength, either in experienced staff or museum or library holdings. That first year (1948) four trustees and two staff members
were on the faculty for the ten days, and the subjects offered
were writing local history, teaching state and local history, early
arts and crafts, history in museums, and collecting folklore.
The response was encouraging in every way, and part of the fun
was knowing that we were pioneering, for so far as we could
learn, no historical society in the country had ever offered this
kind of service.

The next year we hit our stride, meeting for two weeks,
offering ten courses, five each week, sometimes with as many as
eleven distinguished teachers or panelists in one course, all of
them serving only for their expenses. This was the year we offered "American Folk Art" for the first time, with a panel consisting of Nina Fletcher Little, Alice Winchester, Jean Lipman,
Holger Cahill, Erwin O. Christensen, Edith Halpert, and
Mary Allis, a star panel if there ever was one. Again, so far as I
know, this was the first time a historical society had offered a
serious approach to this as yet generally unacknowledged body
of American art; each of the seven panelists was an important
pioneer, as the years ahead would prove. Another innovation
that year was a course called the "Restoration and Use of Historic Buildings," and this has been a continuing area of concern
in the seminars. By 1955 Caroline Keck was giving her first
course in the conservation of paintings; that course and its successors under Sheldon and Caroline Keck's leadership did more
than any other one factor to make those responsible for historical museums and collections in this state conscious of the need
for a continuous awareness of the health and welfare of the
paintings and other objects in their care.

As one looks back over the offerings of the thirty-four
years of seminars, we have repeatedly rung variations on certain themes: the history of New York State; historical societies
and their administration, museums, libraries, publications, interpretation; preservation and conservation; social history;

folklore, folk art, American arts, crafts, decorative arts and literature. In our view all these subjects were part of American
history and parts which we were in a position to interpret. Until the mid 1960s I considered seminars a major responsibility of
my own, then Fred L. Rath, Jr., our vice director, took over the
decision making and leadership, to be followed in the early seventies by our colleague Milo V. Stewart, by then associate director and chief of education. The themes have been much the
same with, in recent years, stronger emphasis on hands-on activities in the realm of crafts and decorative arts. The seminars
still hold a fascination for hundreds of students each year and
have carried word of NYSHA to the far corners of the country.

There was another side to all this. Seminars have been
and still are fun: the sitting beside one of New York's most beautiful lakes, the time spent with others who share one's own enthusiasms, the camaraderie of students and faculty, evening
programs that ran from Honey Coles's jazz dancing to Harold
Peterson's lectures on historic American mixed drinks. As with
the old Chatauquans, a cadre of students came back every year
giving a sense of continuity. If none of this now seems so very
unusual, it may be because, with the ultimate in flattery, others
have imitated or developed their own comparable programs,
which is the way we hoped it would be. In a sense, we at
Cooperstown were helping to redefine the role of the historical
society, a role that today is hardly recognizable from what it
was a third of a century ago.

The concept of The Farmers' Museum had been current
from the early forties, and a number of people were active in its
growth long before I arrived on the scene. Dixon Ryan Fox,
president of NYSHA, and Jared Van Wagenen, trustee, farmer,
and weekly radio broadcaster were both enthusiastic about the
association creating a museum of rural life. Van Wagenen had
made an interesting and important innovation as the person in
charge of the farm tool collection at the New York State Fair,
housed in a building known as the Witter Museum. He had
found, in the 1920s, men and women who remembered the old
crafts, shoemaking, spinning, and weaving and brought them
to Syracuse to demonstrate their skills for the duration of the
ten days of the fair. To the best of my knowledge this was the

first time anything approaching a museum showed the early implements in use. Later Van Wagenen enlarged a slim pamphlet he had written about the Witter collection, called *The Golden Age of Homespun*, into a full-length book (published by Cornell University Press in 1953) covering many aspects of earlier rural and agricultural practices. The title was first used by Horace Bushnell, a Connecticut preacher about 1850, a phrasing which aptly reflected Van Wagenen's rather romantic vision of the past.

Three men on the Association staff were deeply involved in the first stages of planning and collecting the artifacts from the farms of the neighborhood: Edward P. Alexander and Clifford L. Lord, the directors; the other was George Campbell, whom I have already mentioned. As Campbell gathered in these relics of the rural past he listened to what their owners had to say about them, what their fathers and grandfathers had told them. Besides all this he read extensively until he became an invaluable encyclopedia of rural ways and farm life.

Stephen C. Clark, Sr. was also interested in the growth of this project from a somewhat different angle. His brother Edward Severin Clark had been engaged in agriculture and had owned a famous herd of dairy cattle. (It was open to the public on Sunday afternoons, demonstrating the latest in milking equipment and in the sanitary management of the dairy. I remember visiting it in the late twenties.) Mr. Stephen Clark lacked his brother's enthusiasm for agriculture as such, referring to the great stone barn as "my brother's cow palace," but he was devoted to the memory of Edward, and when his associate, Paul S. Kerr, suggested that the dairy barn would make a suitable home for a farmer's museum, a collection for which was already up to five thousand items by the fall of 1942, Mr. Clark agreed, and the plans accelerated. In a short time he had purchased for The Farmers' Museum the collections of William B. Sprague, a founder of the Early American Industries Association, and of Elsie W. Edsall, a collector of spinning and weaving implements who had been a demonstrator at the Witter Museum. Finally he bought the tools which had gathered in the barns and tool house of the Wyckoff family, one of the last surviving farms in the Borough of Brooklyn, going back to

1700. The Farmers' Museum was established as a separate corporate entity but closely allied with NYSHA at every level, with interlocking boards of trustees and with most of the professional staff serving both institutions. This unity made possible much that was accomplished in the years ahead.

One of the first acquisitions in which I shared was the famous Cardiff Giant, that tall tale in stone which had caused such a furor in 1869, the year after it was carved in Chicago and buried in a farm at Cardiff, south of Syracuse. My father as a child of two was taken the long ride by buggy from Pulaski fifty miles to see this wonderful hoax that caused scientists to declare it a petrified man, while the clergy swore it proved the Biblical statement that there had been "giants in the earth in those days." This caper had long amused Mr. Clark, and despite the frown of some of his close friends, he thought it belonged at The Farmers' Museum — as did I, for it correctly stretched the concept of history to include laughter and folly. He bought it from Mrs. Gardner Cowles, and we buried it much as it had been shown in Cardiff, eighty years before.

When I arrived in Cooperstown in 1947, the main building at The Farmers' Museum was already completely installed with exhibits, but of the cluster of subsidiary buildings which were to comprise the village street, only the schoolhouse was complete. The country store from Toddsville was finished but still empty, and masons were working on the smithy. As spring wore on Janet MacFarlane, the highly professional curator, brought together the items to fill the shelves of the store, not easy to do, and never done to everybody's satisfaction. We were keeping our interpretation between the 1790s and the Civil War and to find appropriate, unused items for the shelves of a typical country store was all but impossible, but at last we decided we had gone as far as we could. But there was something wrong. I remembered country stores from my youth, so did George Campbell. It was the smell — there was none of that enticing combination of odors that the very words "country store" evoked. So we spent a good deal of time discussing of what it was comprised. Fresh ground coffee, tea, salt fish, kerosene, tobacco spit on the hot wood stove, some cloves, and a bit of cow manure from customers' boots. All that was available, and we

did our best to get the ingredients in suitable proportions and
properly distributed, then we shut the door at sunset and went
home feeling we had brought historic interpretation one step
nearer truth — and, perhaps in its way — truth's equal, beauty.

Alas for dreams and ambition! I had forgotten one thing.
The next morning a new interpreter of the store was due to take
up her duties — a rather prim, very conscientious lady of later
middle years. I was chained to my desk all morning and most of
the afternoon. About quarter to five, I broke away and went
straight to the old store. The lady was leaving, but I hailed her
cheerfully, asking, "How was it? How did it go?"

She looked at me rather sternly and then said slowly,
"When I got here this morning there was a terrible odor, but at
lunch time I bought four Air Wicks — with my own money,
mind you. By tomorrow it may not be too bad." I learned my
lesson. Never again did I fail to make clear to the staff the whys
and wherefors of changes and innovations. Some of my col-
leagues may think they remember a time or two when I forgot
— but I cannot.

We agreed among us that more buildings should be added
— typicality was a prime consideration. We intended to stay
within a fifty-mile radius, since the development of that area
had been fairly simultaneous. In the next few years we added a
printing office where we printed the little newspaper called, in
honor of the earliest local paper, *The Otsego Herald*, also
broadsides and booklets. A doctor's office came all in one piece
from Westford where it had been used by Dr. Elhanan Jackson,
a typical country physician of the first third of the nineteenth
century. A druggist shop from Hartwick, which had also served
as a doctor's office at one time, gave variety to the growing
street, for it was built of pink, local brick; here we sold soaps,
tobacco, candies, and other appropriate items. A lawyer's office was already on the grounds, for Supreme Court Justice
Samuel Nelson had once owned the Fenimore farm, and his one
time summer law office had become a garage. It was renovated
easily enough, and about that time we were given an early lawyer's library by the heirs of Abraham Becker of South Worcester
which proved to be remarkably complete.

The old Bump Tavern from Ashland, originally built in

1796 and enlarged in the 1840s, was brought in twenty-one seg-
ments which we covered with tarpaulins until the foundation
was ready. One rainy day during seminars, Nina Fletcher Little, dean of the folk art scholars, and some others of us were
crawling around these units when we came to what had been
and was to be again second floor bedrooms and hallway. The
rain had leaked in and the wallpaper was hanging loose. Mrs.
Little reached up and pulled it off the wall, and there on the
plaster was a beautiful example of stencilling. She looked at me
and laughed, for only a day or so before she had asked me if I
knew of any wall stencilling in New York State, and I had trust-
ingly replied that I had never heard of any, doubted there was
any. Within a couple of years we had records of scores, eventually hundreds of other examples — but up to that time hardly
anyone had looked, and you do not find what you do not seek.
Ultimately the tavern was put together again and the stencils
restored, but we left one panel for the curious to see what it
looked like when we found it, covering it with an overlay, a
hinged panel freshly stencilled like the rest of the room.

In the 1790s a fair number of Rhode Island families came
to Otsego County, among them a farmer named Joseph Lippitt
who built a house in Hinman Hollow, six miles from Cooperstown. His descendants prospered, and many continued to live
in the area. In the early 1950s Moses Lippitt gave the museum
that house, which we moved and furnished as a comfortable
farm family might have had it. A log barn of the same period
came shortly after and other out buildings. Oxen, horses,
sheep, hens, hogs, ducks made the place come alive, and the
women guides in the house cooked each day in the open hearth
or baked in the bee hive oven. To give objects life, to make artifacts serve as they were intended to serve, to show the hand skill
with the tool — these were the objectives we sought.

The last building was the church, which came from Cornwallville, not far from Ashland, the original home of Bump
tavern. For ten years all of us involved had searched the back
roads for an attractive, characteristic country church. Over
and over again word would get out here or there that those people from Cooperstown wanted the local church, and a community that had paid no attention to the church or its function

would suddenly come to life, hire a clergyman, and religion would blossom again. For some years I felt like a one-man revivalist. But at last the folks at Cornwallville decided they would rather have their church cared for and used at Cooperstown than let it go the way of so many others — to the bulldozer or become a chicken coop or flea market. Shortly after it was opened on the museum grounds it became again the scene of weddings and musical recitals, religious and memorial services. Twice members of our own family have been married there, and twice we have memorialized those close to us in that simple, godly space.

The innovations by which we sought to make The Farmers' Museum alive and meaningful are now commonplaces in outdoor museums. This was a period when many sister institutions were experimenting with various ways to interpret the past, and all of us borrowed freely from each other. The key to success was sound research, as in any historical project. With it went a desire to give the total experience a human scale, to translate for the visitor what it would have been like to live in pioneer New York.

The collection of Hudson River School landscapes and academic genres of rural life Stephen C. Clark, Sr. had purchased for Fenimore House were for me another new world to explore. All I knew about art I had learned in a two-credit course given at Hamilton by Edward Wales Root, a collector whose genius lay in discovering the future powers of young artists. In my graduate years at Columbia I had learned the joys of visiting galleries, especially one owned by an odd duck who was kind and patient with this ignorant if enthusiastic frequenter of his premises; his name was Alfred Stieglitz. I warmed to the work of my contemporaries like Reginald Marsh (I had first seen *High Yaller* in Edward Root's dining room), John Steuart Curry, Thomas Hart Benton, Grant Wood, and especially Waldo Pierce to whom Stieglitz introduced me. Liking is one thing; knowing is another. So at Cooperstown I set about learning what I could about American art, starting out with introductory volumes by James Thomas Flexner and Edgar P. Richardson, both of whom later became friends.

Fenimore House had a good collection of genres, especially

paintings of rural life in New York State which complemented
The Farmers' Museum. The masterpiece was William Sidney
Mount's *Eel Spearing* in which the shimmering heat of a summer day, the tension of the imperious black woman, the crisp
detail of boy and dog delighted me the first moment I saw it,
and a third of a century later it still speaks to me with no uncertain voice.

With characteristic sureness of taste Mr. Clark had created a relatively small collection of superb examples of landscapes, genres, and portraits, all with a reference to New York's
history or life. Gilbert Stuart's *Joseph Brant* and Benjamin
West's *Robert Fulton* hung with the unique collection of
bronzes cast from J. H. I. Browere's plaster life masks. Cole,
Durand, and Morse along with others of their peers had
painted the landscapes, so that as I studied the history of our
painting tradition I had constant access to examples of the masters of the first seventy-five years of the republic. From the beginning, this became a respite and a joy that offset the day by
day rigors of administration. Later in this volume I shall relate
the story of how there was added to this academic overview the
major collection of American folk art for which Fenimore
House is now famous.

In 1953 I remarried. My bride, Agnes Durant Halsey, had
been in charge of the painting gallery at Harry Shaw Newman's
Old Print Shop and editor of his monthly bulletin *The Port-
folio*, where her articles on folk art had first attracted my attention. She and I shared — and still share — a broad range of interests and points of view with enough separate interests to add
spice. An avid knitter, a superb photographer, a creative cook,
a writer of clean, neat prose, by instinct a scholar, she has the
compulsions of a reference librarian blessed with a sense of
humor and an unquenchable zest for life.

It came as something of a shock to her to learn that I had
never taken a vacation; tactfully and gradually she set about
changing that, but it was a long time before she succeeded in
developing holidays when her workaholic husband did not include some way of propitiating a puritan conscience with one
form of professional activity or another. The first trip we made

to Europe was in 1960; it lasted 100 days, during which we visited 136 folk museums. Oddly enough the marriage survived.

Actually that trip to northern Europe had never been envisioned by either of us as a vacation for we were anxious to compare European folk museums with The Farmers' Museum, and also to see what relationship we could find between the work of the naive painters of the Continent and our American folk artists. The trip turned out to be a watershed in a variety of ways. One night in Bergen, Norway, my close friend and colleague, Fred Rath reached us by phone to say that Stephen Clark had died, a loss I felt acutely. A few days earlier, at Maihaugen, the folk museum in Lillehammer, we had met a curator named Fartein Valen-Sendstad whose concept of folk life and its broad application, its variety of facets, its demands upon the museum personnel started a train of thought which eventually led to the creation of the Cooperstown Graduate Program.

By 1963 the Association had grown in so many ways that it was ready for new adventures. It had acquired the libraries of Carl Carmer, Roger Butterfield, and Harold W. Thompson. A library building was being considered. The staff was strong and professionally experienced. Through the Seminars we had developed a national reputation for adult education. Our junior program, the Yorkers, established so successfully by Mary Cunningham and Clifford Lord was prospering under Milo Stewart. *New York History* continued to hold its own among the academic historical journals, and The Farmers' Museum had continued to grow in size and attendance and especially in the quality of its exhibits under Per Guldbeck's guidance.

My close association with the American Association of Museums and the American Association of State and Local History had led me to observe that nowhere could one get training for work in history museums and societies. The whole museum field was becoming more professional; the roles of curators, registrars, directors called increasingly for specific training. No longer could the retired fourth grade teacher do the job. The public was asking more and more of its museums and historical societies: knowledge of historic preservation, urban planning, an awareness of the problems of conserving art and artifacts, the ability to translate scholarship into terms the average citizen could understand.

My long membership in the American Folklore Society and my continuing correspondence with the leading folklorists made it clear that the professional folklorists were concerning themselves only with the verbal aspects of our traditional culture. I wanted to see a place where one could study those other traditional elements in our society: crafts, hand skills, costumes, textiles, arts, food, architecture — *ad infinitum*. I also saw that education in folk life would provide an invaluable orientation for young professionals in historical societies and the growing numbers of outdoor museums.

I had been thinking about this ever since talking to Valen-Sendstad in Maihaugen, but now it began to shape up. The plans required linkage with one of our academic institutions. For some years we had been cooperating with the State University College at Oneonta. President Royal Netzer and Dean James Frost when approached, were immediately enthusiastic and remained totally cooperative, as indeed, did their successors. Then I sat down with Mr. Clark's successor as chairman of the board of the Association, Dr. Henry Allen Moe, who as director-general of the Guggenheim Foundation had become a leading statesman in the world of scholarship and academic life. Sage, experienced, knowing practically everyone in the world of the intellect, he never forgot that his father had been a master cabinetmaker and that he himself could and did turn out fine woodwork in his shop in Sherman, Connecticut. We had become good friends, and he encouraged and forwarded my planning of the Cooperstown Graduate Programs from the beginning. By happenstance one of the Association trustees was former Lieutenant Governor Frank Moore, now chairman of the board of the State University of New York, and, while the chancellorship was vacant, in practice had become the chief executive officer. With his support the project moved very rapidly, and in the September 1964 we opened our doors to the first class of the Cooperstown Graduate Programs, jointly sponsored by NYSHA and SUNY College at Oneonta.

While faculty from the college and members of the museums' staff taught some courses, we brought in two other professors that first year. Frank O. Spinney, who had been president of Old Sturbridge Village and was now director of the St. Gaudens Museum, came to teach museum administration and decorative arts. From Indiana University came a folklorist and expert in the media arts, Dr. Bruce R. Buckley who molded the folk culture (or as he preferred to call it, the "folk life") program. In 1970 Sheldon and Caroline Keck developed a third program concerned with the conservation of artistic and historic objects which has proved to be an important success.

Looking back over the eighteen classes of thirty students a year, I feel that we have put the rich resources of the Association and The Farmers' Museum to maximum usefulness. Our graduates, spread across this country in a wide variety of historical museums and agencies, have made remarkable records for themselves and for the programs. Their concept of what is historic covers the tapestry of our past, disciplined by a stern sense of sound research procedures and standards. My only regret, and it is a keen one, is that it became necessary to drop the folk life segment of our offerings; but the growing success of the museum studies program is a tremendous satisfaction.

I retired in 1972 and under a grant from the National Endowment for the Humanities, Agnes Halsey Jones and I had the opportunity to sample American folk art wherever we thought it was to be found in the United States or Canada. Travelling in a motor home for a year, we covered seventeen thousand miles in twenty states and two provinces. We recorded all manner of traditional folk arts in 62 private collections, 105 museums, 14 outdoor or folk museums. Mrs. Jones took five thousand photographs of fifteen hundred objects; those slides became the nucleus of our archive of American folk art owned by the Association, now numbering somewhere between twenty and thirty thousand slides. These are constantly being used by scholars and in our team teaching of American folk art at the graduate program. In the years since retirement it is folk art that has occupied our minds and energies — enough to sharply season these more leisurely years.

For the rest of this volume, we have selected articles which reflect my search for a better understanding of the way the unsung citizens of this state have lived and worked and played and died. To paraphrase Robert Frost, I have lived to see a road less traveled by become a highway full of young scholars seeking the same understanding.

New York State and Its Heritage

T HE first two pieces which follow are expressions of the love affair I have had all my life with upstate New York. I trust that years of travel have given me enough perspective to escape provincialism while remaining a regionalist. My overview of the state was written as a foreword to *A Short History of New York State* by David M. Ellis, James A. Frost, Harold C. Syrett, and Harry J. Carman, published and copyrighted by Cornell University Press in cooperation with NYSHA in 1957. It could be noted that history, folklore, and material culture play a role in this foreword as they do in "Land of the Upper Hudson," written for a special issue of *Antiques* devoted to the Upper Hudson in July 1951. There is some kind of magic for me even in the names of New York's four great rivers: Hudson-Mohawk, Delaware, St. Lawrence, Susquehanna — Susquehanna whose birth at the outlet of Otsego Lake I have monitored from my bedroom window each morning for a third of a century.

Anyone involved with any historical agency today faces decisions as to what we should save — architecturally — and what we should let go down the drain. In the late 1960s and early seventies as vice chairman and then as chairman of the New York State Historic Trust, I learned more about preservation than I knew in 1955 when I wrote "A Look at Historic Preservation"; but my point of view never changed very much. The occasion for the article was a conference called "Historic House-keeping," sponsored at Cooperstown by the National Trust for Historic Preservation and NYSHA. My co-chairman was Fred L. Rath, Jr., director of the trust, but by 1956, when *Antiques* published papers from the conference, Mr. Rath had joined us in Cooperstown as vice director where he was an invaluable colleague.

Perhaps the most significant aspect of the article "Three Eyes on the Past" is the date, 1956, when it appeared in the spring and summer issues of *New York Folklore Quarterly*. Recently scholars have been citing it as foreshadowing studies in American folklife. In any event it represents my thinking as director of The Farmers' Museum and influenced my thinking when we were planning the Folk Culture Program at the Cooperstown Graduate Programs. Its intent was to be provocative rather than comprehensive.

Foreword to A Short History of New York State

FROM the beginning we in New York were many peoples. After the Leni-Lenape came the Iroquois, a confederation of conquerors and conquered. On the heels of the first Dutch settlers, men sailed in from across the face of Europe; four decades after Hudson's voyage eighteen languages could be heard on the streets of New Amsterdam, and more were being spoken all the time. When the English raised their flag and changed the name to New York, the flow of strangers did not stop. From Africa and France, from the little duchies along the Rhine and the cities of the Italian peninsula, from the ghettos of Portugal they came to find a corner for themselves in the New World. The English tongue borrowed from other tongues and British ways absorbed other ways.

These men and women coming on the four winds brought with them the limitless hopes and gnawing fears of all mankind. For some the hopes eroded away on stony farms or in fetid sweatshops, and the fears became realities, but for others and their children the hopes and fears gave strength to action, to protest, to law and change, and their dreams came to life in the land.

If the people were various, so too was the land to which they came: the sandy stretch of Long Island pointed a remem-

3

bering finger to the sea they had traveled, and the valley of the Hudson, with its proud Highlands, its purple-cloaked Catskills, its gaunt Adirondack crests, formed the first highway. Many other rivers were here waiting: the Mohawk was found early, and later the Genesee with its great falls, and the knotted, moody Susquehanna that married us forever to Pennsylvania, the Salmon and Black, the Unadilla and Sacandaga, and, on the far border, the Niagara plummeting four inland seas into a fifth, and, finally, the river of the North Country, the St. Lawrence. Rolling hills and lush valleys cried out for a plow that they might give forth corn and apples, wheat and flax; forbidding swamps were found which even in much later times are left to the wild fowl who relish only solitude. Forests abounded — and they still do — millions of acres of evergreens and hemlocks, oaks and elms, and, most gratefully discovered, the maple, the tree that sweetened the pioneer's porridge and gave him his first crop in a resisting wilderness.

If the rivers were roadways, the lakesides were refuges and oases of serenity. The winters were tempered on their shores, and the summer breezes whistled through the young corn. There were fish there and laughter for boys swimming white and glistening in the brightness. There were lakes no bigger than a banker's parlor and lakes ninety and a hundred miles from source to outlet, lakes inland lying like the fingers of a giant's hand, and others bordering Canada and stubborn Vermont.

This is the state with a show start; it did poorly under kings and royal governors. The bungling rulers in Whitehall and St. James made decisions for New York on foggy days, while here a rich few held the fertile earth and the powerful streams tight in their jeweled hands. Only under the surface did the yeast of freedom work silently, with now and then a bubble bursting the surface calm — Leisler's seizure of the government, Zenger's attacks in his press, the rebellion of the men of Flushing, and black slaves rising in terrible anger. As the second century moved toward its great drama, the yeast worked more actively — Sons of Liberty, Prendergast and his down-rent farmers, the tea party in Manhattan — but by and large the people were docile, touched with lethargy, their fears tugging ever at the coatsleeves of their hopes.

War came and much of it was fought over our fields and in our woods. There were defeats here — Brooklyn Heights, White Plains, the lost battle for the soul of Benedict Arnold, and the burned villages of Springfield, Unadilla, German Flats, and Cherry Valley; there were hard-won victories at Oriskany and, the most far-reaching of the war, at Saratoga.

Following the peace, a new spirit moved across the valleys. The veterans with their brides trod on the heels of speculators who dealt in thousands of acres. The sweet song of the ax and the soft tread of oxen transformed a forest into cornfields, and soon the retted flax, broken and hatcheled through the magic of strong, young fingers, grew to thread, then on the loom to homespun for britches and diapers, always diapers for the big young crop that would clear more land and harvest more grain and go still farther west.

Ships by the thousand found the snug harbor at New York, and the tills were full of money from the West Indies, from Spain and London and tortured France. Roads unwound in place of trails, and talk grew of canals — Mr. Washington himself had recommended one. Men quarreled about the constitution and balanced in their hearts the dangers of a federal union against the greater dangers of loose confederation. The spirits of men stood straighter, and the Revolution, which had sometimes seemed so meaningless, became a turning point, a bold release of human spirit.

All the pent energies burst into flower. New Englanders, pouring across the disputed borders, over the Hudson, through the valleys, brought changes and in turn were changed. The freer air of New York released them too, and the towns they built were raised with a difference, subtle but unmistakable. Their daughters chose German names for their children, and their sons found good the blue-eyed Irish girls, and a new nation of born Americans went to schools for which all the people paid, and they read the books and papers cascading from the ever-growing number of hand presses. They had opinions, strongly held. In the ebb and flow of politics, of change and skulduggery and reform, they inched their way forward. More and more men went to the polls, and fifty years after Saratoga the last slave in New York was free.

The women too moved up, noisily sometimes, gently at others, standing ever closer and surer by their men. Here Iroquois women had once ruled their tribes and spoken to be listened to in council — perhaps something of this clung to our earth and infected our air. We have come to fancy this breed of women with their blunt truths and their speaking out in meeting; confident men are not abashed by confident women.

In that half century after the Revolution the Empire State came into its own, and the capstone of its progress was Clinton's Ditch, dug by hand from Waterford to Buffalo. Where crossroad villages had sprawled lazily, suddenly cities sprang up and then factories and all the good and evil of great towns. Amsterdam, Utica, Syracuse, Rochester, Buffalo — the mules plodding on the towpath brought the wide world to their gates, and they flourished. People going west and wheat coming east — the bloodstream of a nation flowing ever faster. Back in the hills, too far to the south or north to benefit, other towns of promise withered on the vine as coal replaced the great mill wheels. Then the railroads once more altered the pattern, and still another growth set in, with wide-funneled puffers speeding up life, changing the pace, adding new towns, new ways, newcomers. More tongues to be filtered into English, more ways to mold with ours, more young muscles to be party to the building and the growth.

Yesterday, like today, was not all bathed in sunlight. There are shameful passages and dark stains on the wide pages, the cheap crooks, the character assassins, pullers of strings, the calloused in high places and low. But we have been lucky in the long run of years, for we have raised up in every generation leaders who shone through the worst murkiness of their day, the Clintons, the Livingstons, Jedediah Peck, Grover Cleveland, William Seward, the Roosevelts, and Al Smith with his rough speech and his greathearted vision. And there are others, to the end of a long folio, men and women who could not be bought or tamed or forced back into their places. Blessed be their names, including all those long forgotten or never known beyond the village caucus.

Land of the Upper Hudson

FOR miles through the silent mountains the trickle flows — a vagrant brook playing at the feet of mountains — from the beginnings to the sea, guarded and shadowed by mountains.

Cabins and shabby farms lie beside it — housing men to whom guns and a rod are dearer by far than the hoe and the plow. There are singers among them and fiddlers and builders of tall and magnificent lies. And there are old chests in the darkened corners and rockers so long in the family they're known by the name of some ancestor, for all else forgotten. And beside them, all higgledy-piggledy, the newest devices from Montgomery Ward.

It widens and deepens — a brooklet grows into a river. Thus it was flowing when Burgoyne and his regulars met the long rifles at Old Saratoga and a tide that was drowning a stumbling rebellion was halted. Jane McCrea knew the river — and thought of her red-coated lover, never suspecting her scalp lock would cry out to Yankees and Yorkers for vengeance and stir to a blazing the smouldering fires of the forest. And Dame Schuyler, setting a torch to her wheat fields lest they should nourish the British, added her footnote to history, her hammer blow to forging a nation.

Beverwyck, Fort Orange, Albany — the trappers coming in from the forests — the silent Indians with furs on their backs — the Dutch burghers piling the pelts in their steep-roofed houses — changing the fashions in Holland and Paris. The silversmiths followed the money; the suave grace of their spoons added beauty to tables laughing with victuals and brews. The weathercock over the First Church saw the little stockaded village sprawl up the hillside. Pinkster Mondays he watched dancing Negroes dressed in their gayest, the wild African rhythms beating on State Street and Market, while Dutchmen and English stayed home — peeking out at the mystery of slaves become men for a day.

Thus far the *Half Moon* had traveled and on one of these sand spits Kidd buried his doubloons and diamonds and a dead boy to watch over them. The whalers came out of Nantucket and settled at Hudson. Sperm built their houses and their womenfolk watched the bend of the river, waiting and waiting — fearing and waiting as the women of seafarers ever must do.

Up in the hills at New Lebanon the Shakers offered their hands to work and their hearts to God, dancing, like David, before their Lord. Their great farm prospered while seed and herbals were sold to a nation, and the prim beauty of their furniture was like one of the younger sisters, graceful and useful, offering no hint of frivolity — only devotion to function.

To the west, the voluptuous Catskills, purple to indigo, majestic, mysterious, haunting — among them young Washington Irving went wandering — into the dorps that huddled by killsides. From the talk of the idlers in taverns came Rip and the players at nine-pins — thundering, rumbling over the Hudson.

Young Thomas Cole, that ambulant artist, toting his pencils and sketchbook, trudged into identical mountains — the forest was deep in its darkness, the sunlight brightened green patches. He captured the mountains, but more than that happened. The mountains, the valley, the river had captured the first of the painters to love them, and paint them. Happily, there were others to follow.

And while you're about it, consider "Toot" Fulton, painter and crackpot inventor of submarines and other horrendous devices. It was August of eighteen and seven, hot, with a wind blowing southward. At five miles an hour *The Clermont* chugged up the river, her smoke like the plume of a knight in full armor. Both going and coming he laid over at "Clermont," home of Chancellor Livingston, his friend, his Maecenas. His heart lifted — with Harriet Livingston soon to become Mrs. Fulton, with Albany now but a day and half from New York — and steam had come to the river.

Two presidents sleep in the valley, both of them sons of the Dutchmen, and one could remember his grandfather singing the song for Dutch children, "trip trop a troontjes." The voices of Holland left names to remember: Kinderhook, Rhinebeck, Claverack, Moordenerskill, Kaatskill. Not Poughkeepsie — the Indians left us Poughkeepsie; not Germantown, where the Palatines tarried before they set forth for Schoharie and into the Iroquois country.

The Dutch left us houses, still standing some of them and the Huguenots, too, have bequeathed us their little stone cluster at New Paltz, a corner of France but transplanted. Much later, romantical, gothical cottages of Andrew J. Downing set a new style for the country, a style that was known by the name of the river.

Much changes over the decades: the brick kilns are rotting into decay, the wheels of the potters at Athens are lost or rotted away, the Day Line and Night Line no longer come north of Poughkeepsie. But still the shad run in the spring, and the ducks drop down in the autumn, and the apple trees send forth their fragrance.

The hills do not change nor the hearts of the river folk neither. They like to quote Captain Hudson, who wrote in the log of the *Half Moon*, "As fine a river as can be found . . . and pleasant a land as one need tread upon" — the words hold and time has but tightened their meaning. Truly, as pleasant a land as one need tread upon.

A Look at
Historic Preservation

DOES all this fuss and feathers about old buildings that are outdated and have served their original purpose really matter, or is it just an outlet for neurotic antiquarians on the local committee who want to bask in the reflected glories of their pioneer ancestors? In the world of shopping centers, high-speed thruways, and decentralized industries, of what earthly use is the old brick mansion, redolent of yesterday, which occupies the best possible site in town for a gas station? We can't stand in the way of progress, can we?

The answer, of course, is "no." There are times when the house should come down and the gas station should go up. But progress goes from some place to some place, and if we would know where we are and where we are going, we must also keep a few points on the chart to indicate where we have been. Out of this knowledge should come a valuable kind of personal security such as a child is given in a loving home, or such as comes to those who find peace in one of the historic religions.

The past should have as many personal ties for each of us as possible, for none should feel that he is floating in time, rootless and unrelated to all that has happened to our fathers and to those who lived in our place before us. To feel a part of the progression of mankind is to enter into full citizenship in the

11

race of men. In the framework of the home let there be hand-me-downs from yesterday — pictures and furniture or a piece of lace from the old country or the trunk that landed at Ellis Island. Things that have been in a family a long time have a magic of their own, asserting the values of life and its survival.

So it is with each village and city. They, too, need focal points of affection, of the historic community spirit. The variety of these places can and should be numberless, each suited to its own history and people. In a very real sense these should be shrines where the spiritual values of our people are cherished and nourished. In a land where few of us live in the town where we were born there is an ever greater need to create a sense of identity and belonging for those who come from elsewhere. If we have to make this consciously rather than receive it as a birthright, well and good, let us do so as truthfully and skillfully as possible.

Given a historic house that has meaning for a specific town, what are we to do? Put back the original furniture, reproduce the wallpaper, train a guide in costume, and do a historically complete job of recreating life as it was once lived? Yes, if we can do that well and also make the house into an active, functioning part of community life, constantly interpreting as many sides of the past as possible in terms the people of today can understand.

And if this is impossible, shall we do nothing? Shall we tear it down and build the gas station? I'm for trying a lot of other possibilities first. Civic organizations or individuals can be encouraged to buy it, making what changes they must, but accurately preserving the exterior; there are values for a child on his way to school just in knowing that this house stood on this same site when his great-grandfather was a boy, even if that grandsire lived far across the sea.

Between the fully revitalized historic house, which is currently our ideal, and the preservation of the architectural shell, which is the least we can hope for, there are hundreds of possible compromises any one of which might be the solution for a specific community.

This raises the question of whether bad preservation is better than no preservation at all. Strongly as I believe in scholarly standards of research and veracity of presentation for historic houses — and I consider these of vital importance — yet I must admit that there are times when a holding operation is better than destruction; time itself may produce workable solutions. I can think of a number of historic houses which, twenty years ago, were just being held together physically; a growing public interest and new concepts of historic preservation have made these into vital forces for the best kind of interpretation of community tradition.

Finally, what shall we save? Frankly, I'm getting a little bored with the lengthening list of handsome residences of the "best people." We need to preserve buildings that speak directly to those of us whose families had callouses, as well as to those who had carriages. It's a fine thing to exhibit the aesthetic best out of the past, but it can be equally important to interpret the ways men and women worked and created and played. I want to see more gun shops, millineries, schoolhouses, covered bridges, taverns, foundries preserved for our people. Let's speak to Americans in terms that add meaning to their own everyday lives, that place their jobs, their responsibilities as citizens and parents, in historic context so that they see their present problems, not as exceptions, but as continuations of the challenges faced by their forefathers.

People need places out of their past which they can see and understand and ultimately love, that symbolize those who lived in these places before them, and struggled and suffered and built there. If those men and women could face and solve their problems, so can we. We need such refuges all over the land, as we need churches and schools, that they may be seedbeds for the cultivation of a vigorous and informed love of country.

Three Eyes on the Past

FOR the better part of two decades I have worked and played and corresponded with hundreds of people interested in writing local history, collecting folklore, and in creating regional museums of history. All too often these able and conscientious workers operated with no awareness of how much they have to teach each other, how inter-related are their findings. Their results are often piecemeal when a broader view would provide a far more significant canvas on which to read our past.

Despite the tons of books on the history of the American people there remain areas of abysmal ignorance, especially in the realms of everyday life, in the history of our mores, viewpoints, ethics, homes and family life, economics, communal institutions, and the relationship of the sexes. These are also aspects of contemporary life which are under constant scrutiny as we seek solutions to twentieth-century problems. For an understanding of these matters in contemporary life we must have, as we do not now have, a comprehension of their historic roots. The bases of such insights as we seek on a large scale must derive from local studies over a wide geographic spread and back to the beginnings of our communities.

The time has come when writers on local history and culture must use all the resources known to historians, folklorists, and curators if they are going to achieve a well-rounded concept of the past as it was lived by the general run of Americans.

15

With the historian, they must search out not only the obvious printed records but go far beyond that thin vein to find diaries, letters, ledgers, day books, local almanacs. With the folklorist, they must listen to the oral traditions, recording them accurately, considering always the significance of what they hear to him who tells it. They must learn to probe gently, patiently the mind of the teller until everything of value is brought to the surface. And always there must go on a process of evaluation, whether the student is considering the printed or written or oral word; his mind must be both open and critical, open to every possibility, critical of every source, fully conscious of human frailties, yet never blind to the nobility of the human spirit.

And then there are *things*, the clutter left by the past, which are keys to it when properly understood. The common attitude of historians toward museum objects is one of superior unconcern. One can understand their lack of enthusiasm when confronted with an artifact touted as Washington's small clothes, for most of us no longer are greatly impressed by contagious magic. What the historians all too seldom recognize is that this may be an important item in our social history, important not because the father of his country wore it, but because we know so little about the history of what men wore that any item which we can date accurately, from a known stratum of society, is worthy of our study.

What historians have failed to recognize is that there is today a whole school of museum professionals who are working in terms of collections depicting social history, not "association items" often of spurious authenticity. Nor am I thinking only of the great folk museums like Greenfield Village, Old Sturbridge, and The Farmer's Museum. All over the country there is a growing number of enlightened curators of local museums who are collecting and preserving the tools and implements, the textiles, clothing, paintings and carvings, toys and furniture of the average citizens of yesterday. The local historian or the folklorist who does not relate these artifacts to his researches is ignoring a resource of inestimable value.

Indeed, it seems to me that we must borrow the techniques of the anthropologist and correlate all these evidences in coming to a fresh understanding of seventeenth-, eighteenth-, and nineteenth-century America. It is unfortunate that American social anthropologists, by and large, have ignored the Americans who arrived after the Indians, for anthropological techniques could easily and very profitably be adjusted to produce thorough and enlightening studies in local social history.

One area of research now crying out for attention is the frontier and immediate postfrontier period. In chronology this will vary from the seventeenth to the nineteenth century, depending on what part of America we are discussing. Perhaps some general observations ought to be made about this period. First of all, there is the juxtaposition, even on the frontier itself, of extremely diverse ways of life. The primitive and the sophisticated, the well educated and the illiterate were together in the forward march of our people. This is evident in what neighbors read or did not read, in their taste in clothes, food, architecture. We need far more study than we have yet had in the matter of the social stratifications of our frontier and postfrontier society.

Folklorists have tended to ignore the extensive circulation of newspapers, almanacs, builders' guides, songsters, books of recipes, and home remedies. Much of what flowed easily in the oral tradition had come but recently from the printed page. Many a "traditional family recipe" or popular tall tale which we have thought of as having been born and passed on in the oral tradition was derived from a cook book or a popular almanac. If historians need to consider and utilize our folklore, it is equally true that the folklorists need to do research in the printed materials available at an early date.

Another factor to be kept in mind is the mobility of our people. Every generation makes its own move, seeing greener pastures elsewhere. This and the wide variety of our origins (as old graveyards testify) made, indeed still make, for a remarkable fluidity and diversity of our folk culture in contrast to the rigidity of cultural patterns in Europe. One of the never-ending fascinations is the impact, interplay, give and take of acculturation. Families from Europe were constantly being Americanized but, in a sense, the communities to which they came were by a small degree Europeanized by their coming. Despite these varied origins, there is a great common denominator in our folk ways due to this restlessness of our people who not only went west, but north, south, and east.

In certain European countries, notably Sweden, Finland, Ireland, and Germany, pains have been taken to collect in an orderly and scientific fashion the body of information necessary for an understanding of the folkways and structure of their societies. In Sweden, especially, the folk museums and universities have been the centers of research into every aspect of peasant life as it has been lived in all parts of that country. The "Swedish Folklore Archive," which is based on a far more extensive concept of folklore than Americans have had to date, surveys every discernible detail of life. The outline of an archive such as this is of little use to Americans for two reasons: first, it has grown out of the highly specific understanding of Swedish life; secondly, our researches into comparable fields in this country are so infantile and disorganized in comparison that they are not applicable. We must work out for ourselves guides to the study of our own folk life.

I would like to suggest, in the following pages, what may be considered a start toward such a guide. No reader is to think of this as anything more than tentative suggestions addressed to more active scholars who will, I can only hope, find what I have to say worthy of elaboration and experiment. I suppose I have been especially influenced by my studies of central and western New York State from the end of the Revolution to 1850, a period of hand skills, migration, gradually lessening isolation but generally unsophisticated culture patterns. However, I have tried to eliminate the more provincial elements of my scholarly experience so that these suggestions can be of use elsewhere and for later and earlier periods. One point, however, I wish to emphasize: the kind of enquiry envisioned here is dependent upon scholarly researches in the library, upon inquiries among the living memories of the aged and a full analysis of the oral tradition as it was taken down by earlier students, and finally upon a study of the objects left to our times by the past, objects to be found not only in museums but in homes, attics, barns, junk shops. It is in this way that one hopes to bring to bear a fresh triangulation upon our past, to develop a new comprehension of our local history.

What I want to see is a new kind of local history that considers not alone the political and institutional development of a community but which really tells us how Everyman lived, the details of his work day, how he courted, loved, married, raised his family, accepted his responsibility in the social patterns of his time, and what he thought about these experiences. The novelists have done a better job than the historians in these matters; it is time the historians spit on their hands and did the digging themselves.

As an example of the kinds of quest I would suggest, we might look at the field of personal relations and family life, covering such matters as social stratification, love, courtship, the development of the home, the roles of children, manners, the houses themselves, food and drink, the part old age and death played in the patterns of life, and the values by which people lived. Other possible areas to be analyzed would be aesthetic and intellectual strivings, social and civic relations and, finally, occupations.

PERSONAL RELATIONS AND FAMILY LIFE

Social Stratification

One of the oft-repeated myths of American history is that ours was once a classless society. Men have confused the fluidity of our social structure with a lack of structure; probably men in America moved from class to class with greater ease than anywhere else in the world, but stratifications existed and need to be understood.

Some questions one might ask one's self in this matter are the following: Who were the top figures in the community, and were they real leaders therein? What advantages over the run of men did these figures (and/or leaders) have: money? land? brains? physical strength? strong, clearly defined characters? leadership? What were the symbols by which we recognize the head men of a community: size of their houses? carriages? officership in militia? their clothes and that of their wives? accoutrements of the home—piano? carpets? curtains? pictures? the church they attended and the position the family held in that church?

What were the successively lower steps on the social ladder? How can one identify these classes, and how did life differ at each level? By what signs did men recognize that one of their number was on the way up? Who dined or visited whom? And how did all these matters shift and change over the years, increasing as the later nineteenth century progressed?

Of especial interest is the question of who comprised the lowest class. What was the attitude of the group toward the latest comers, with particular reference to the immigrants from foreign lands? What were the local prejudices in these matters as regards race, religion, speech? Local histories generally have ignored the first-comers of such groups as the Negroes, Irish, Jews, Germans, Italians, Slavs. In the long run these group pioneers ought to be remembered and the reasons for their coming placed in the record. For example, who were the first Poles in Buffalo, and why did they choose that city? Or the first Irish in Albany? Pioneers kept coming long after the frontier had moved westward.

These questions (and I have only suggested a few of them) of differing culture patterns at different levels of society must be asked in all the sections which follow. For example, what did people in a particular village put on the walls of their rooms to decorate them? What kind of pictures did the banker buy, and what did the tenant farmer's wife cut out for her delight? What songs were sung in the squire's house, and how did they differ from the songs the blacksmith sang? Mozart was played in the same villages as was "The Arkansas Traveller" — but by whom and under what circumstances?

Love and Marriage

In a society where the family is the core social unit, the relationship of young people as they progress toward the rites of courtship and the wedding are of major importance.

A Proper Match

What did people consider a suitable pair? What similarities of background and viewpoint were deemed necessary, and what deviations were permissible? What was the normal difference between the age of the man and woman? What barriers were created by differences in religion, place of birth, social class? For example, did a young man court and marry the hired girl; if so, what was the attitude of his family and neighbors? Was that considered quite a different matter from his sister marrying the hired man? What taboos were there about consanguinity, and how rigidly did they operate? As always, what differences were there in these matters at different social levels?

Courtship

Consider the social occasions at which young people met and came to know and admire one another: bees of all kinds, church and church socials, dances, parties, sleigh rides, school. And on these happy times what patterns prevailed? Did the boys come by themselves and stay by themselves until the evening had long progressed and then slowly drift toward the girls, or did they come in couples? And how did they go home, in groups or pairs, quiet and orderly or boisterously laughing or singing?

The period of trial and error, or precourtship indecision is the period when the ancient rituals of divination are brought into play. What traditions survive that can safely lead us to reconstruct the ways young people sought to determine whether they had at last met their future partners, e.g., the plucking of daisy petals? What charms were favored for securing the desired one? What types of contagious and sympathetic magic were used? What taboos were honored lest the budding romance be blighted? Hundreds of such beliefs have survived into our day, but what we usually lack is the knowledge of which were thriving at particular times in specific communities and how seriously they were regarded by those who followed them. One also wonders about the aesthetics of courtship, the factors which made it a special and memorable prelude. What gifts did a young man bring his lass? Did he pick her flowers or buy her pretties at the store? What part did music play in their love affair? Did she sing to him or he to her, or did they sing together, and what types of songs seemed fitting to the occasion? Were instruments played? There is evidence that one of the great common bonds with many couples was their religion, but how common was this, and what were the interests of those who were not drawn together by their faiths? In short, what were the simple, important ingredients which went into a courtship?

Betrothal

What was the accepted method of proposal? Did most men "pop the question," possibly on their knees, or did couples drift into an engagement? When did engagement rings or their equivalent enter our scene, and in what ways did a community acknowledge an engagement? And how long, under normal circumstances, did an engagement last? The division of the actual preparations for the new home offers an interesting study. Many wedding chests have come down to us, but we know relatively little about what women put in them, and how much of that they made themselves and how much was given them. The ancient practice of dowry (that wonderfully sensible arrangement) varies greatly from time to time and place to place and requires specific research.

We know little about the more intimate relations of our ancestors, but one wonders if betrothal admitted of greater liberties. Involved is the concept of a woman's "honor" and the emphasis placed upon it by some communities.

Valuable sources of information about the period of courtship are, of course, love letters and diaries, but often one finds that what is left unsaid is of as much significance as what is committed to paper. Silences must be weighed along with what was written.

The Wedding

There is a rich lore about the taboos and rituals surrounding the wedding itself, but again the problem for the researcher is to identify the observance of these at specific periods in the past. The matter of the bride's dress deserves careful note; there were vigorous beliefs about various colors of this gown; one might question at what date white became generally accepted.

Such customs as the bridal veil, "something old and something new, something borrowed, something blue," and the taboo against the groom seeing the bride before the ceremony should be watched for. These are only the hardiest of many other customs which have faded away.

The composition of the wedding party is important and an indication of the intensity or looseness of family structure. Who gave the bride away, and what relation was the maid of honor, the best man, the bridesmaids? Where did the wedding take place—at home or in church? If a clergyman did not perform the ceremony, who did?

After the ceremony what foods were served? Was there a wedding cake, and what were the traditions about the frosting or the kind of cake? Were tokens baked into it? If there was no cake, what took its place? With what liquid did they toast the bride? As temperance overtook the hardy drinking habits of the frontier these customs changed, and their change is a kind of weathervane.

Researchers should keep an eye out for any details about the wedding ring, the bride's bouquet, the send-off, if the wedding night was spent away from the place of marriage. The wedding trip itself seems firmly rooted in our folk ways, and after 1825 a wedding trip on the Erie Canal to Niagara Falls became a kind of dream which thousands of young couples hoped to see fulfilled; but many people went merely to the next town staying but a day or so, and, of course, many of them, caught in the seasonal rush of spring or early summer, went nowhere.

Finally, what kind of a welcome did the community give the newly wedded pair? Were there hornings or shivarees? Was this just a noisy occasion or was it a roughhouse? One of the interesting evidences of this custom is the clapper and the horse fiddle still occasionally found in back country attics or museums.

Establishment of the New Home

Another question of vital importance in the understanding of our early familial patterns is the question of whether the young couple lived with his parents, with her parents, or whether they set up a new home of their own. In many instances where the young couple stayed on with the old folks it affected the architecture, ultimately causing wings to be built on the older houses. Involved also is the question of whether or not the land was sold to the young couple by the parents, whether the family acres were divided up under clear titles of new ownership; whether father and son or father-in-law and son-in-law worked the land together. Certainly this must have differed from family to family in the same community, but there will be areas, I am convinced, where it is possible to find a discernible consistency. If one may be permitted a broad generalization, capable of a great many qualifications, one would say that in Europe the tendency was for the young couple to live with the older family and that the American tendency was for the young people to start out on their own; but there must have been many deviations from this, and perhaps there were many, many alternate arrangements worked out, all of which we need to see in perspective.

Children

A first test of any people is their attitude toward children. Did a young couple aware of a forthcoming child rejoice, or did dark fears destroy the pleasures of their creation? To what extent did their attitude reflect the fertility or sterility of the land, the availability of land, a rising or falling economy? The relative importance of boy babies and girl babies: was one preferred? What reasons were given? Was the preference limited to the first child? How important did children seem to the community? Was a good deal of thought devoted to them, both in the home and the community at large, or were they ignored?

Pregnancy

Ask what beliefs about pregnancy were widely held, for this is a phase of life that almost always generates a special folklore of its own. Of note are the beliefs predicting the sex of the child, prenatal influences, and the diet and taboos for the mother. Consider the layette — the first clothes a body possesses are of special interest. Few enough have come down to us, but occasionally a little bundle will be found which fate caused to be unneeded. The attitude of husbands and other men in the community toward the pregnant woman is one indication of the place of women in a society, frequently an indication of whether they were accepted realistically, romantically, or negligently.

Childbirth

Some houses may have had a "borning room," but little enough has been recorded about these. Was it usually on the first floor, near water and kitchen fireplace? The presence of neighbor women and of a qualified midwife to preside over childbirth was usual before doctors were available and, indeed, in some areas long afterward. In terms of the history of medicine we need to know more about the procedures of these women and how they differed from those of the physicians. Casual observation leads us to believe that the death rate of mothers and children at birth was high, but this whole area requires careful research at a local level.

Babyhood

The names that parents choose for their young reflect not only the two families that are joined by a marriage but also religious, political, and social enthusiasms. Certain names are popular at certain times and then go out of fashion. The tendency to keep the mother's family name alive is important from any number of points of view. The ritual of infant baptism should be watched for, and all kinds of birth records deserve the most careful preservation; these will be found on the "family history" page of Bibles, on colorful frakturs, in diaries, and even account books and recipe books.

There were certain rituals relating to very new babies: for example, that a baby should be carried *up* stairs before it be carried *down* so that it will rise in the world; that during the first year of life it should have neither its nails nor its hair cut with steel scissors lest it "steal" when it grows older. These examples only suggest an extremely fertile field of research.

What were the possessions of babies? What were their very first toys, their clothing, their furniture? We have trundle beds, cradles, cribs, walkers, tiny chairs, potties. Who made these, and what were their models?

Attention should be paid to the feeding of infants. When nature's own solution failed, other methods had to be found, and one should watch for nursing bottles and flasks, pap warmers, pap boats, baby spoons. We need to know more, too, about the foods that graudally replaced milk in their diets.

Preschool Years

In some ways the most important questions we can ask are those with the most elusive answers. What, for example, was the emotional climate in which children were raised — one of joy and laughter, of gentle sternness, of acrimony and neglect? While this differed from house to house, yet communities very early develop standards which distinguish between desirable and undesirable attitudes. It is these standards which the local historian should try to recreate by striking some sort of average based on the information available to him.

What games did adults play with the very young? "Patty-cake" and "This Little Pig" and their equivalents are the first steps a child takes into the narrative and theatrical arts. All the little songs that are sung and the stories told to amuse, to pacify and edify are the beginning of an individual's culture pattern, and a valuable index to the cultural values of a community. This aspect of folklore is often considered negligible, even by folklorists, who ought to know better. One should also watch for the first prayers and the first proverbs children learn from their elders, nor should the student be surprised by an utter lack of consistency of viewpoint which these findings will reveal.

We have been discussing matters which children learn from their elders. But very early they learn from their slightly older brothers, sisters, and neighbors and become attuned to the mores of the young. They learn all the games, shibboleths, taboos, fetishes of the young. These represent an ever-increasing complexity until they enter the adult group. These range from ball bouncing rhymes to group games to the moral code of the young group which may bear little observable relation to that of the adult group in the same community. Every local historian and folklorist should reread *Tom Sawyer* every eighteen months to keep his sights clear, for no book I know gives us a better awareness of the child world and its folk patterns.

Chores and Sports

As part of their education, children of both sexes were given chores, often at a very early age. What were these, what was the attitude of adults and children toward them, in what order did they progress? Similarly we should watch for the child's growing participation in sports — swimming, fishing, hunting, trapping, wrestling, running. Who taught him, his father, or other boys? Was he taught with ridicule or patience? What comparable activities were there for girls?

Manners and the Code

What kind of manners were children taught? Were the relations with adults invariably formal? Modes of address, such as bowing, rising, hat tipping, curtsying need recording. But more important is the moral code that was taught or implied. What differences were there in the code which was taught to children as desirable and the real actions of their parents? Many a storekeeper's son, for example, was taught a code of honesty which was at sharp variance with the day-by-day dealings of his father.

The relationship of children and their parents comes back, ultimately, to the question of whether people think of each other as individuals or as stereotypes. Did the adults who looked at Johnny see a highly individual personality or A Child? The answer to this will give clues also to the group's attitude toward class, race, and religious relations.

School Years

The school as a community institution will be treated in a

later section, but it might be useful to consider it here from the child's viewpoint.

The distance from home to school must have loomed large in the minds of many early American children, especially in the northern winter months. The discomforts of hard seats and a stove which heated only those parts of the body facing it, the smell of wet mittens, the luncheons brought from home, the fear or friendship of older students, the placement of benches and desks in relation to the stove, the teacher's desk, and the light all need evaluating. Consider too, the personality of the teachers who represented, in some communities, the best, in others, the worst, and punishment and rewards, the games played at recess, and the folklore communicated.

Folk Pediatrics

The subject we might call folk pediatrics has had very little research as a phase of medical history, but we need to know much more than we do about children's diseases and treatment. Asafoetida, goose grease, and hundreds of other folk cures were standard procedures, but they have seldom been treated as a phase of the medical history of a community. The exception that comes to mind again is a novel, Samuel Hopkins Adams' *Canal Town*. The cures for warts are legion and seem to have been frequently passed along at a child level. Statistical studies of children's ailments can be approached by way of physicians' account books which often prove most illuminating.

Gangs

Boy gangs and clubs in both urban and rural life offer an untapped subject for research: the structure of the group, bases for admission, qualities required for leadership, activities, rituals. Related to this, at least indirectly, is the youthful attitude toward adults in general and parents, teachers, police, clergy in particular. There is also the question of how children (and adults) considered and treated children of other races and religions, their attitude toward the blind, cripples of various kinds, and all those who failed to conform in the ways to which they were accustomed.

Sex Education

We know very little about the history of sex education where it existed largely as an element of folklore, yet its importance for the understanding of our adult patterns is incalculable.

School Age Art

One segment of American folk art is concerned with the work of school girls, and a community should be searched for watercolors, frakturs, memorial pieces, needlework, theorems, and related work done by girls from eight to eighteen, some of which is of a very high quality and all of it of interest historically. Besides the pieces themselves, printed curricula of the local schools and surviving textbooks may offer valuable leads. Boys seem to have concentrated on calligraphic art or steel pen drawings which were deemed more manly and more practical in a period when good penmanship opened so many job opportunities.

Clothing

Relatively little clothing for young people has survived either in family collections or museums. However, examination of contemporary paintings gives us a general guide, especially for the more comfortable classes. By the second quarter of the nineteenth century, the genre painters were leaving records of the clothing of all classes of Americans, including children of poorer families. Pinpointing this kind of detail to a particular community may not be easy, but a searching eye often discovers the forgotten and neglected.

Manners

The topic of American manners has been a lively one since the days of Mrs. Trollope. Certainly this is a place where there were, in the eighteenth and nineteenth centuries, vast differences among the various classes and in different parts of the country. It is safe to say that American manners differed from those of Europe, although, so far as I am aware, no comparative study has been made.

Basically one could approach this subject with the yardstick of an individual's consideration for his fellow men, for this is the core of good manners. But beyond this are all the amenities and complexities of human relations, only a few of which we can suggest here.

The first question one must ask is how important good manners seemed to the people of whom we are writing. Was this one of the ways strangers were judged, was the calibre of manners associated with social acceptability?

What were the forms of introduction and greeting? Under what circumstances did men bow, raise their hats, shake hands, and when did women curtsy?

What forms of address were usual: between men and women, husbands and wives, men, women, children and adults, employer and employee? What special or honorary titles were used, e.g., "Judge," "Captain," "Colonel?"

Table manners should be noted, and there was a whole spate of amenities in relation to snuff taking and smoking.

The degree to which spitting, chewing, drinking, sneezing, nose blowing, belching, scratching were taboo or acceptable is a guide to the relative importance of manners. On a slightly different level is the use of profanity, which involves certain moral values, and such manual profanities as nose thumbing and related insults.

Finally one must consider the difference created by the presence of women in any given situation. What actions and what words were taboo when the opposite sex was present?

Ethics and Values

We have considered the ethical teaching of children, but the larger question of human values demands attention. Ethical values are not static; especially is this so in a society as fluid and mutable as ours. What was good in one decade was not necessarily good in the next; the movement to the west of community leaders, the influx of new racial stocks, the decline or increase of prosperity, the changes from rural to urban life could, along with any number of other factors, bring basic changes in the patterns that men considered good or bad.

Moral Code

What was the moral code which one might consider an average for the community, and how far and to what extent were there deviations from this? This concerns not only the relation of the sexes but all social and business relations. What were the values given to such key words as "good," "bad," "honest," "dishonest," "sharp," "loose," "virtuous," "chaste," "duty," "pleasure"? Consider the emphasis upon a man's "word," and all the kaleidoscopic changes to be seen in "honor," both as applied to men and women.

Popularity and Unpopularity

It might be useful to diagnose the men and women who were popular to determine which of their qualities seem to have been desirable constants. Similarly one could analyze those who were unpopular to find the qualities that seemed undesirable to their contemporaries. Another sidelight on this subject can be found in trickster tales and hoaxes. Not only are the incidents themselves illuminating, but the attitude of the community as reflected in them is even more so. It seems to us that there was considerable cruelty in frontier America, but it was a cruelty which, as they say in the theater, often had the "consent of the audience."

Beauty

If sharpness and cruelty require scrutiny, so too does the attitude toward beauty. What were the criteria by which one judged a woman beautiful or a man handsome? Were people aware of the delights of nature and landscape or were they blind to them? What attention was paid to color and decoration within the house? How did women "pretty up" their homes? Did they plant flowers near their houses and, if so, what varieties did they choose?

Emotion

What were the accepted expressions of emotion? Was there considerable laughter and gaiety? Did women weep frequently, and what was the attitude toward the tears of men? What expression did anger take and how commonly was it expressed? Consider profanity, its range, its frequency, its imaginativeness and the taboos which operated against it.

Folklore in New York State

I HAVE already written that from 1940 to 1946 I taught a course in American folklore at what is now SUNY Albany in which students collected folklore still current from their families and neighbors. All of those reports are now in the Folklore Archive at the NYSHA library and provided the source material for articles in this section. Collectors and informants names are available there.

"The Ghosts of New York: An Analytical Study" was published in the *Journal of American Folklore* in the October 1944 issue. The articles on the Devil and werewolves were written under a grant from the Guggenheim Foundation and published in the *New York Folklore Quarterly*, in the spring 1952 and fall 1950 issues, respectively. "Practitioners of Folk Medicine" was first read before the Section on Historical and Cultural Medicine of the New York Academy of Medicine in January 1949, then it was published by the *Bulletin of the History of Medicine*, September–October 1949, and reprinted in the sesquicentennial issue of *New York State Medicine*, February 1957.

One must remember how long ago these materials were collected. I don't know what one would find today, covering the same ground, but I am very conscious of a rebirth of the attention paid to witchcraft, spells, haunted houses, werewolves, and a whole range of unpleasant supernatural manifestations in popular books, movies, and television. I'm not sure there are more true believers, but certainly more people evince interest than did forty years ago.

I have often been asked how I became interested in the folklore of the supernatural. Well, it was not because I was a believer—I was not then nor am I now. It was because in those early days of the folklore movement, except for my good friend Wayland Hand out in California, almost nobody else was putting his or her mind on this aspect of our field. Half the fun lies in pioneering.

The stories and beliefs represented here are a reminder that New York State has always had a remarkable mix of cultures. Folklore in New York was constantly enriched as the later immigrants told their children and grandchildren tales of the old country. It has been this way since the seventeenth century.

The Ghosts of New York

AN ANALYTICAL STUDY

WHEN a newspaper publishes a current item of ghostlore it does so with something between a snicker and an air that signifies amazement that anybody still believes in ghosts. On the other hand, material in my archives indicates that the people, whether they are believers or not, still enjoy telling of the experiences of the restless and returning dead. My first interest was in one type of story that kept reappearing – the vanishing hitchhiker. The publication of three pioneering studies of California ghostlore and of the vanishing hitchhiker by Rosalie Hankey and Richard Beardsley (*California Folklore Quarterly* 1, nos. 1–2; 2, no. 1) encouraged me to make a rather extended analysis of all types of ghostlore current from 1940 to 1944 in New York State.

While a number of ghost stories have been published in New York collections, I have ignored these to concentrate entirely upon the ghostlore items garnered by my students in an undergraduate course in American folklore and now deposited in the NYSHA library. Most of the students were collecting for the first time, and more experienced collectors might often have gathered further details which would have been useful and significant. Be that as it may, the students and I have collected four hundred and sixty items of ghostlore from all over the state, except New York City, from every social stratum,

35

from nearly every racial and religious group in the state. It is perhaps significant that one-third of the folklore collectors found some ghostlore, and that the four hundred and sixty items came from two hundred and twenty-nine informants.

Certain groupings of the material to which reference will be made should be kept clearly in mind. These stories were collected both from people whose families had long lived in New York State and from families recently come from the Old World, consequently four-fifths of these ghosts are Americans and one-fifth Europeans. For obvious reasons it has been desirable to make distinctions between these groups, but only where there were significant differences will special notice be taken of the origins. The ninety-six stories with European setting represent twenty percent of the total, but among these were found only twenty-six motifs of which there were no American examples in the collection and six of these belonged to another special group, the Sicilian and Italian buried treasure lore.

Two types of story, because of their popularity and peculiarities, demand special notice: the buried treasure lore and the lore of the vanishing hitchhiker. The thirty-six examples of buried treasure lore involving a ghostly guardian are equally divided between our native folklore and the folklore of Sicilians and Italians. While there are other minor differences, the chief distinction appears to be that in America treasure so guarded is never possessed by those who seek it, while in the Mediterranean it frequently is.

The vanishing hitchhiker, who has been treated so extensively by Miss Hankey and Mr. Beardsley, is the central figure in the most popular ghost tale in America. This is the story of a driver who picks up a young woman hitchhiker and takes her to her home, only to discover when he gets there that she has vanished from the car. People in the house identify her as their dead but restless daughter. The archives contain forty-nine examples of this story, its forerunners, and closely related types. In my attempt to reach some generalizations in the pages which follow I have been forced to take special notice of this group, from time to time, lest elements within it distort by their frequency the true picture of current ghostlore in New York.

The following analysis, then, will be based upon stories

orally current in New York State (exclusive of New York City) between 1940 and 1944. In the files of the archives is information which gives us the name and background of the collector, the name, origins, age, occupation, and address of the informant of each item. Where this is significant it will be drawn upon. In an attempt to offer a comprehensive pattern for the study of ghostlore I shall discuss appearance, purposes and character, when and where ghosts return, activities, and folk attitudes toward ghosts.

APPEARANCE

The returning dead may choose one of three possible forms: first, he may appear so lifelike that unless one knows from prior knowledge that this person is dead or unless one sees him vanish, he is mistaken for the living; second, he may reanimate his corpse; or third, he may appear in a spectral form of some sort. These are the possibilities for appearances, but it should be remembered that many ghosts are never seen but known only by their deeds, the noises they make, or the mischief they commit.

Approximately a third of all our ghosts appear lifelike. They are easily recognizable by those who have known them and appear to have changed not at all from their living state. A common type of story is a modernization of the account Daniel DeFoe wrote of Mrs. Veal who visited and chatted at length with a friend without the latter realizing that Mrs. Veal had been dead for some hours. Of course if the living know of the revenant's death — and this is the usual situation — we are less certain of the absolute versimilitude of the ghost to his living form. Living persons are reported as recognizing their parents, children, sisters, brothers, sweethearts, wives, husbands, friends, enemies, and neighbors. In this group of stories the common experience is recognition of the ghost by the living, beyond all peradventure. Many people meet ghosts whom they did not know when alive, and frequently they would never be aware of the fact that these are ghosts if they did not disappear into thin air before their eyes. Characters of all ages, races, religions, and in a wide range of distinguishing costume (soldiers, sailors, gypsies, Quakers, for example) appear to strangers and, after their errand is accomplished, leave the living in open-mouthed amazement as they literally fade out of sight. While it cannot be claimed that all of these revenants were so lifelike that they would have been mistaken for the living if they had not been known to be dead, or had not disappeared, it does appear to have been the case with a large proportion of them, and all of them were vivid enough to be recognizable to their beholders.

The living corpse is not a ghost, but it is one of the returning dead. Such a one has been certified dead but acts momentarily as one of the living. There is body and substance to his form, but it is a dead body. Most commonly the corpse moves, sits up, climbs out of the coffin, or speaks to the mourners. Several of this group are either from Ireland or told by Irish-Americans about an American experience.

When we begin to analyze the less clearly envisioned revenants we become aware of a change in terminology. Whereas these we have been discussing are invariably called "ghosts" or "the dead," the words now used reflect a less clear concept of the experience in the mind of the informant. "Apparition," "presence," "spook," "spectre," and "shrouded spirit" are all reported. Classification is possible, however, because these wraiths are characterized by either whiteness or by lights. In this subdivision of spectral ghosts I have also included ghostly parts of the body which function by themselves. All told, these spectral ghosts will account for approximately twelve percent of the whole.

The descriptive phrases which now concern us are as vague and indistinct as the phenomena to which they refer. The commonest phrases are "white ghostlike shape," or "large gray shape," or "wispy white mist." One child was "surrounded by a nimbus," while other spirits were called "hazy figures" or a "white shape." Despite the airiness of their appearances they can run, yell, lift beds, lead the living to their death, and other normal ghostly activities. One who disappeared with the smoke up a chimney is an exception.

The lights which are so common in ghostlore appear to be of two quite different genres. One is, as it were, the guise of a returning spirit, the other a supernatural phenomenon with some unique significance. The first group are sometimes informative, leading one to the hidden burial place of the ghost, who had been murdered. Others move about in houses they inhabited, or in cemeteries. In old Fort Ontario, a generation ago, a mysteriously moving light was believed to be the soul of a soldier who had walked the post in his lifetime and continued to do so. The darting balls of fire for which the scientists have no adequate explanation are believed by some to be ghosts, by others, merely supernatural lights which carry a warning of impending tragedy. This latter explanation they share with several other types of light. For generations one family has been warned of approaching death by a group of lights, very much like a lighted birthday cake, which wander about the fields a day or so before the death. This is not considered a ghost, but simply a supernatural light. Two other examples of the appearance of flames in connection with ghosts ought not be omitted. One version of the story of the Horseman of Leeds tells of a woman who sits on a rock with a lighted candle on each finger. And a Polish story describes a ghost appearing in the room in which she died, completely surrounded by a ring of flame.

Irving's *Legend of Sleepy Hollow* which he heard in Columbia County near Kinderhook and transplanted to his native part of the Hudson, has made Americans generally conscious of the tradition of the headless ghost. The archives contain fifteen examples of this motif, none of which bear any marked evidence of Irving's influence. Four of them are European in origin, coming one each from England and Ireland, and two from Sweden. Two of the New York stories are concerned with the digging of buried treasure; one of these is of Negro origin. Another story from the Helderberg area concerns a headless Negro ghost, and still another concerns a headless Indian. With one exception the native ghosts are men, but two of the Europeans (one English, the other Swedish) are women. Four of the headless ghosts ride horses, as did Brom Bones, but there is considerable evidence that this is merely a continuing tradition from which Irving obtained his inspiration. All the headless ghosts

seem very real and are spectral only in the sense that being in-
complete they could hardly be mistaken for the living.

From German informants comes a story of a floating head
which informs a man of his sister's death, and we also have the
face of a lover poisoned by his sweetheart which illuminates itself on a tombstone on a rainy night and says, "I loved her, I
loved her." A golden face which appeared at a window, like the
floating head, warned of approaching death. Bloody hands appear annually on the door of a house near Pittstown to commemorate a murder done there years ago on that date. From
long strands of hair fished out of a mountain lake came a ghostly
voice which told of the owner's murder, the details of which
were very like the Brown-Gillett case upon which Dreiser built
An American Tragedy. Perhaps the most imaginative story of
this group comes from Negro informants and concerns a ghostly
set of limbs, torso, and head which bounced downstairs, assem-
bled themselves, and then chased home a courageous fellow
who was trying to spend the night in the haunted house. As he
caught up with the living man he asked, "And what fault do
you have to find with me?"

If we exclude the hitchhiking ghost from our calculations,
the predominance of male ghosts over female is striking. The
sex of unrecognizable spectres is practically impossible to determine, but among the stories where the ghost appears in an approximate facsimile of its living form, the male ghosts are almost exactly twice as frequent as the females. This proportion
holds equally well for European ghosts told about in New York
State as for our natives. The contemporary stories of the vanishing hitchhiker almost always concern a girl or young woman,
but probably in the earlier form of the story the rider was a
man. In better than half of the total number of tales at our
disposal the sex of the ghost is indeterminable due to lack of evidence or to the vagueness of the form of the ghost.

In the matter of age there is a general lack of information.
Only when the revenant is very old or very young does the informant mention the age. Roughly speaking, one ghost out of
ten is the spirit of child or youth, and generally these died
deaths of violence. Not only is the proportion of adult ghosts
who met violent deaths not nearly so high, but these figures are

also interesting in view of the high mortality rate, from "natural causes," among children and youths a relatively few decades ago. Once more the vanishing hitchhiker must be left out of our primary calculations, but its inclusion would increase considerably the number of youthful revenants and the number who met violent deaths, since frequently she died in an auto accident.

The aged are specifically mentioned occasionally, but the bulk of the stories assume the ghost to be middle aged or neglect the detail. In all but one story a ghost is the same age as the person was at death; in the exception an old father who had long been decrepit, came back to lambaste his daughter's suitor and appeared younger and far more robust than he had been at the time of his death.

Whole groups of recognizable ghosts frequently appear together. Always these revenants have had something in common during their life times. An occasional couple wanders in the same spot they loved, and there are at least two New York families that recongregate in or about the old homestead. One family on Shelter Island has elaborate parties with many toasts and great hilarity. These parties are at their best when a fresh recruit has joined them from the land of the living.

Some servant groups return together. In old houses where Negroes were mistreated their spirits are frequently seen. One house which served as a station in the Underground Railroad is haunted because the cellar where runaways were hid caved in and buried a number of them together. Another pathetic lot are some girls in Schenectady who were being held by a white slave ring when, for some reason known only to the proprietors, the girls were murdered. To the Schenevus Valley return Indians and the white settlers they murdered.

Some groups of revenants worked together in life. Three orchestras continue to play earthly music despite their passing over; one of these orchestras is Italian, one Irish, and one rides up the Harlem Division of the New York Central Railroad on a flat car attached to Lincoln's funeral train. Army officers and their men, sea captains and their crews, and three bridge builders who were killed during the construction of the Mid-Hudson Bridge (together with their cat) return to former scenes of action.

Certain others who found a kinship in religion or death keep each other company on their visits: mourners, people who died in the same hang yard, three who died violently in the same hotel, a carload of insurance sales men killed at a railroad crossing, and inhabitants of the same graveyard. In passing it is worth noting that in the entire collection there is only one instance of a group of graveyard ghosts, although individual revenants appearing there are fairly common. There are both Jewish and Catholic stories of midnight religious services in which the entire congregation has come back from beyond.

A common errand may bring a group together. From Sweden comes an account of four headless ghosts who return to take a living man back to their bourn with them. In Pennsylvania is a house into which three came trooping occasionally to hunt for clothing they had left behind.

In the democracy of death there seems to be no group which escapes restlessness. Those who were devoted to religious works are as likely to return as those who lived the most execrable lives. As a matter of fact, the archives contain more stories of returning clergy than returning sinners, unless some rigid moralist insist that we add the unhappy suicides to the latter group. The largest single occupation represented are farmers or members of farm families, a fact which is a reminder that ghostlore, while to be found in both city and country, thrives better in the rural areas. Business men — usually rich ones, bankers and stockbrokers — are fairly common. A special group of tradesmen, the peddlers of the last century, form a sizable bloc, largely because so many of them were murdered for the money they carried with them. Among industrial workers railroadmen are most likely to return, but other occupations, such as tannery workers and bridge builders, are represented. Among the professions the clergy are prominent, the physicians and teachers are not uncommon, but the lawyers are, to all appearances, abiding in some place from which it is impossible to return. Two frequently reported types of story increase the number concerning clergymen. The first of these has Irish analogues and is found in New York State among the Irish-Americans. It tells of the priest who has forgotten or been unable to say masses for the dead for which he has been paid, and he returns to his church to do this. The other type is one version of hitchhiking ghost stories in which the revenant is a nun.

Many of the older stories concern disreputable characters. Stories about a slave trader, or a horse thief, or a pirate will go back, probably to the times when such occupations were fairly common. Some ghosts are spoken of in general terms as having "died bad," or as having been criminals or drunks or gamblers. In Schenectady is a piano player who earned his living in a brothel—and who keeps right on playing years after his murder.

Soldiers and sailors are frequent revenants, and every war brings on a fresh crop of stories—and this war is proving no exception. Both Negro and Indian ghosts have been seen in New York State, being further evidence of the lifelikeness of many of our ghosts, for pigmentation would be difficult to determine in a diaphanous wraith.

Tales of ghostly animals fall easily into two groups, those in which the animal is the ghost of a man appearing as an animal, and those in which the spirit of the animal returns in its own guise. Human ghosts borrow the form of dogs, snakes, white horses, white goats, and in one instance, of a rose-breasted bird. One notable fact is that out of twelve such examples, five of them are Italian, two of whom appear as dogs, two as snakes and one at different times as both a white horse and a white goat. In general, the activities of the Americans are much the same as those of the Italians. The ghost who comes back as a snake (American) returns to watch his property and is fed regularly by his family. A Negro girl told of her grandfather's spirit coming back both as a dog and as a goat.

Approximately one story in every ten has some ghostly animal, the commonest being horses and dogs. The horses frequently are drawing ghostly vehicles, hearses or carriages, or carrying riders, half of whom are headless. One story which is rather unusual tells of a Hudson Valley farm where they had had the same team of horses for many years so that all the harnesses were double. When one of the beasts died the hired man was hard put to it to adjust the leather in such a way that it could be used by a single horse. One evening as he struggled to fix the harness for a two-horse cultivator, he saw Old Dolly rise out of the ground just over the spot where she had been buried.

She ambled over to her old place ready to complete the team. Later he reported, "The skin was a mite loose, but it was Old Dolly, all right."

The dogs are both seen and heard barking. One of them took it upon himself to guard innocent working girls as they went home late at night through the less desirable section of Haverstraw. Another, a white poodle who had been murdered with his mistress by her husband, always accompanied the lady when she came back to visit the old home. Supernatural, although not necessarily ghostly, dogs frequently guard treasure and come growling into view just as the diggers locate the box. One would expect that cats with their mysterious ways, their unexpected entrances and exits, would tend to return, but only two are on our records. One of these would run right under the nose of a dog who was "bad on cats," and he seemed not to realize it was there. That cat could walk through a closed door, the only animal ghost I know to have had that habit. Ghostly cattle and a bird complete the list of ghostly animals.

Reciters of ghostlore tell you frequently of inanimate objects which reappear at the same time as do the ghosts themselves. Thus a ghostly murderer wheels in a ghostly wheelbarrow the ghostly corpse of a man he killed long ago. In other words, scenes are completely reenacted, and this involves certain paraphernalia that has never been animate. While this is not a new motif, yet it is worth pausing to consider. If ghosts are the restless souls of the dead, what of these trains and wheelbarrows and hearses which no modern religion would claim had ever had souls? It may be a continuum from much earlier times when souls were not denied inanimate objects, or it may be another example of the illogic found so often in folklore.

The ghostly conveyances are almost always old fashioned. We have no record in New York State of a ghostly plane or automobile, tractor or streamlined express. We do have one ghost train on the Harlem Division of the New York Central, but its mid-nineteenth-century, crêpe-draped engine draws only two cars, a flat car with an orchestra on it, and another car containing a flag-draped coffin. It sounds like Lincoln's funeral train which has been reported in the west, but what ghostly dunderhead has switched it off the Hudson River Division, where it belongs, and sent it up the Harlem Valley? We have ships, but they are the vessels of the early Dutch explorers, and our hearses are horse drawn. The Irish Dead Coach, lacking as it does in Ireland the horses to draw it, used to go the rounds of Cohoes, taking in the souls of the day's dead. Perhaps the earliest of our vehicles is an Indian canoe, paddled by a chieftain in full regalia.

When a ghostly Quakeress appeared to a Troy maiden, the furniture actually in the room faded out and was replaced by older, simpler furniture, and differently placed in the room. After the little Friend had searched through each drawer she and her furnishings disappeared once more. Any night a wee ghostly skeleton was to be seen in its cradle in a hidden room in a Johnstown cellar, but never were they visible in the day time and even at night if one put forth a hand, the whole scene vanished. Knives, clubs, shovels, musical instruments were brought back by many a ghost, but only one ever took anything away with him, and that was a cheery old man who was so delighted to find his accordian in his nephew's room when he came to call that, after playing it for a spell, he decided to take it with him when he went.

Some objects are heard but not seen: dice are heard to roll; music, but especially violin music, is heard; and silverware and glasses are heard to tinkle — all these when no human hand was near and often when no such articles were within reach. Most intriguing of these stories is one about a house in which beleaguered travelers spent a night with a pleasant pair of hosts. Because the hosts were poor the travelers left a fifty-cent piece on a marbletop table when they departed early in the morning. In the next town people told them there was no such house any more, nor any such people as they described—though all admitted that there had been, long before, such a couple, now dead and buried, and such a house, now a heap of rubble and ashes. So the perplexed travelers returned to find the driveway overgrown and only a gaping cellar full of burned timbers and refuse. One curious item they did locate — the cracked and sooty marble top of what had once been a handsome table. On top of the dust was shining a fifty-cent piece.

PURPOSES AND CHARACTER

The evidence available indicates that something more than a third of our ghosts died violent or sudden deaths. The largest number of these were murdered, and while murderers seldom return, the victims of murder seem particularly restless. Accidental deaths account for almost as many ghosts as murder. They died in various ways: drowned, killed in battle, in duels, fires, railroad and automobile accidents (the vanishing hitchhiker very often died this way), in industrial accidents, and at the end of a hangman's rope. Another active but unhappy company are the suicides. Since no one, anymore, bothers to bury them at crossroads with an oak stake through the heart, they wander over the land, as morose, as unhappy as they were in their latter days.

A clue to this emphasis upon sudden and violent death may be found in a belief expressed by a Sicilian informant that those whose natural lives are interrupted in this manner must wander until the natural term of life has expired. Thus Sicilian robbers murder a young boy and bury him with their treasure so that he will be on hand to guard it as long as he normally would have lived, at the end of which time his spirit may rest.

In a great many instances it is impossible to fathom the reasons why a ghost returns. His purposes may be clouded, the story may not contain sufficient details at the point at which one hears it. Often all we know is that such a house is haunted by ghosts in such a manner. However, certain patterns do emerge when a sufficient number of items are collected, and they can be classified.

(a) Ghosts come back to complete unfinished business. This may be some lost article, often of trifling significance to the living, which the ghost feels impelled to find. Fathers of posthumous children return to see their offspring. Priests return to sing masses for which they had been paid. Others seek to comfort their loved ones, to hunt their decapitated heads or missing arms or legs, to see to the paying of their debts, to ask forgiveness, to obtain reburial, and a variety of other tasks they could not complete when living.

(b) They warn and inform. Frequently it is to foretell

death, or to announce their own deaths to those far away from them that they return. They tell or try to tell where money is buried; they advise the living in making decisions.

(c) They punish and protest. Faithless lovers, disobedient children, intruders, the ghost's murderers, thieves, agnostics, card players, drunkards may feel the presence of a displeased ghost, and may feel it pretty forcibly, too. One returns and will return until justice is done his name, while others annoy the tenants of their former homes.

(d) They guard and protect. They keep watch over buried treasure, they protect their children or the innocent and virtuous; they cause damaging evidence to be destroyed; they warn people, often unknown to them, away from dangerous places.

(e) They come back to reengage in their lifetime activities. Some go fishing, those who were hungry or thirsty continue to look for food or water, some play their musical instruments, continue to hunt for buried treasure, another annually rides over his farmlands on horseback, while an Indian chief keeps on looking for his wife who ran off with another brave.

(f) They come back to reenact their deaths. One man who died putting on his pants has been seen several times by his relatives going through the same awkward procedure until he drops over as he did at the end of his life. The suicides do it all over again, and our Horseman of Leeds drags his victim over the Green County roads.

(g) They reward the living. This is a very small group, and all of them are Irish or Italian. These are rewards for kindnesses or for courage.

The traditional reaction to ghosts is fear. In the folk narratives where the ghost hoax is perpetrated this expected response is usually found. In the comic sheets, in the folkways observed throughout the country on Halloween, in radio horror programs, it is assumed that a ghost will terrify. I want now to examine the evidence to determine the mood displayed by ghosts in their visits as recounted in our ghostlore to determine if this fear assumption is justified. This is not an attempt to determine the character of those who return, but rather the dominant attitude during their visits. I find that revenants are either indifferent (fifty-eight percent), malevolent (thirteen percent) or benevolent (twenty-nine percent). These categories are entirely subjective, based upon my judgment of their actions.

The first observation must be that over half of the revenants are neither friendly nor unfriendly toward the living but supremely indifferent to them. Into this classification falls almost every example of the vanishing hitchhiker, which tend to swell the percentage somewhat, but even without these stories it would include fifty-two percent of the lot. These indifferent dead come for some minor purpose of their own and pay the living little or no heed. There is an austerity, a terrible dignity, a deep abstraction which gives them an air of thoughtfulness. They are neither sad nor glad but preoccupied.

The ghosts that annoy and are more of a nuisance than a danger should draw our attention here. The poltergeist may have any one of a thousand motives for his knocking, clanging, tapping, furniture moving, bed cover pulling, and general nuisance making. Some of these actions are to attract attention so that the ghosts may impart information, or bring to pass one or another of their purposes, but an equally large number are totally indifferent as to the impression they make upon the living, and their visits can be classed as neither malevolent or benevolent.

Malevolent ghosts deserve careful consideration because of the widespread attitude of fear noted above. All told there are five stories in the collection (four hundred and sixty tabulated) in which a ghost causes death. One of these is Italian, one Irish; of the three New York State ghosts one brings his thieving son to suicide, one kills the assailant of an innocent girl; the third avenges the desecration of his family's graves by causing the death of the child of the desecrators. More frequently they wreak physical violence upon those they hate; branding, scratching, knocking down, whipping, beating are some of the commoner forms this punishment takes. Almost never does a ghost hurt a person unknown to him, almost never does he act without cause. Innocent bystanders are frequently frightened, but it is only a rare ghost who will do them harm.

Many ghosts come back in the best and kindliest frame of mind. They are helpful, consoling, rewarding, informative, or penitent as we have already seen. Even, occasionally, they are in a lighthearted laughing mood, but these are rare.

It should be reemphasized that the figures do not substantiate belief that ghosts need universally be feared. Those who have harmed the dead may well take care, but anyone with a clear conscience is as safe with a ghost as with one of his neighbors.

WHEN AND WHERE GHOSTS RETURN

The student of ghostlore is confronted with a variety of problems when he tries to pin down his stories in terms of time. First he must determine when the man died, then the date of the incident which is being recounted. It is a rare day that he finds the answer to both of these questions. Not infrequently inferred details within the narratives are a help in determining the first of these problems. A fair number of ghosts had some connection with historic events: Indians during the French and Indian War, soldiers of the Revolution, Negroes in the days of the Underground Railroad; or they were historic figures themselves: Captain Kidd, Martin Van Buren, Aaron Burr, Dr. Guthrie, the discoverer of chloroform as an anesthetic. One is all too frequently met with such answers as, "Oh, this guy lived a long time ago," or, "He was alive in your great grandmother's time," or, "before the war" (which may turn out to be the Civil War or it may not). The fact is that unless the narrator has a personal, family, or historic interest in the ghost he is very unlikely to know when he lived.

It is somewhat easier to determine the date of the ghostly incident being recounted, but here again vagueness predominates. There is a scattering of dates from the early eighteenth century to the last quarter of the nineteenth century; from then on to the immediate present there is a steady flow of stories. For twenty years the vanishing hitchhiker has been appearing in every corner of this country. Now the people are telling of the ghostly homecoming of soldiers and sailors of World War II who have been killed in the far reaches of the war fronts.

Three-quarters of our reports indicate a single appearance of a ghost; if it came back again or elsewhere there is no mention of it. The remaining quarter are quite explicit in their statements regarding the frequency with which the revenants make their appearance. About half of these have made repeated visits at uncertain intervals, these being described by such terms as "repeatedly," "occasionally," "frequently," "three nights running and before that, too." Another sizable group are those ghosts which return at regular and predictable intervals such as every night, every afternoon, every day, every week, Saturday night, midnight, once a year, "first thing every morning." Others come on a certain date or occasion: The anniversary of the death of the revenant, Christmas time, "one certain day in April," "August 15." Another small group come back under special circumstances: rainy or moonlight nights, whenever someone tries to dig treasure, when a woman needs protection, when it thunders, whenever a man leaves his wife at home all evening while he goes to play cards with his friends, whenever death is coming to a particular family.

A little better than half our stories indicate the time of day at which the ghost appeared, and it may surprise some to learn that nearly twenty percent were seen during the daytime. No ghost gives any indication that he must hurry off at cockcrow; as a matter of fact, five are up and about in the early morning hours. Just half as many appeared at precisely midnight as during the daytime, but nighttime is, as the daytime percentage shows, by far the favorite time for the restless dead to wander. No season of the year seems to be favored, but rainy and moonlight nights are fairly popular.

While ghosts are as likely to be found indoors as out, they do show a decided preference to country over city life. Those who haunt houses, and about a fifth of them do, tend to choose some one room in a house which is their favorite. Anywhere from the cellar to the attic and the stairs between may be chosen, frequently for good cause. It may be the scene of some catastrophe in their lives, it may have been a favorite spot, it may be the place some valuable (or for that matter, worthless) personal possession was left behind. A number of them hang around outside in the yard, in the swimming pool, near a filled-in well, beside the front gate, while others go farther to the barns or orchards, to the fields and fences beyond. Even after a fire, ghosts will sometimes haunt a blackened foundation.

Many of our ghosts are found along roadways — all of the vanishing hitchhikers and many others besides. Bridges are not only not taboo but fully as popular as cemeteries. Marshes, ponds, lakes, rivers, islands, woods, seashores are all known to have been visited by ghosts, but roads, cemeteries, and bridges are outstanding in their popularity. A scattering of industrial sites should be mentioned: railroad yards and tracks, tanneries, a cheese factory, a slaughterhouse, and a store. Of the public buildings churches and forts are most likely to be visited, but schools and hotels have their visitors too.

I am convinced that the findings we have examined so far are not very different from what will be found in other northern states. I want to turn briefly to the special problem of the geographic distribution in New York State of these stories, for that too may be useful to other collectors when they come to translate these findings to the problems of their own sections. We are concerned here with native ghosts only.

Remembering that these stories were collected by students in my classes in folklore one would expect that those counties most heavily represented in the class would be most heavily represented in the ghostlore collection, because every student tried to get all the different types of folklore in his home community. But this expected correlation did not develop except for those counties which lie along the Hudson and Mohawk valleys. Of the ten counties which contributed the greatest amount of ghostlore, nine were on one or the other of the valleys, and the tenth county (Otsego) lies just south of the Mohawk. In other words, New York State's native ghostlore is most readily found on either side of the Hudson Valley from Newburgh to Troy and along the Mohawk Valley from Cohoes to the section around Utica. This is our oldest settled region, the inhabitants of which originally were Dutch, English, and Palatine Germans and are now very cosmopolitan with sizable admixtures of Irish and Italian. The valleys were settled when ghostlore was universally believed, and in recent years immigrants have frequently just left lands where belief in the supernatural was part of the climate of opinion. Three other sections of the state are important in this connection: the Adirondack Mountains and parts of the Catskills, which while sparsely settled and only slightly represented in this collection, have much good ghostlore yet to be collected. The Schoharie Valley, as Miss Gardiner has shown in *Folklore of the Schoharie Hills*, is also rich. Perhaps as significant as anything else are the areas from which little or no ghostlore was collected. Long Island and the Southern Tier (counties bordering on Pennsylvania), while amply represented among the collectors, made almost no ghostlore contributions. For ghostlore to thrive one needs a section that has been settled for a considerable length of time, where the houses are old, and at least a fair share of the population is permanent. This provides for the localizing of stories in particular houses and permits the material to thrive among a people who are familiar with the families involved. Very often our informants begin: "You know Jerry Brown — well did you ever hear how his grandfather used to come back to that stone barn of theirs?" Narrator and listener are on familiar ground, and the story sticks and is passed on to another generation that knows Jerry Brown's children and have slid down haymows in that barn. One of the tantalizing problems is why some long-established communities with a relatively stable population just don't have ghostlore. I am thinking, for example, of the Charlotte Valley, south of Oneonta. Within a few miles on the north and northeast are towns like Milford, Cooperstown, Worcester which are rich in ghostlore. All the perceptible factors are favorable, but the ghostlore isn't there. Perhaps there has been some hard-headed, realistic element in the minds of enough people to discourage the survival of this material.

The ninety-six stories in the archives told of European ghosts by people of European origin are predominately Italian (forty-two) and Irish (twenty-six), but Poland, Sweden, Great Britain, Finland, Russia, Germany, and Armenia have all made contributions. One of the striking lacunae of the collection is Jewish ghostlore, which I find is very rare. After diligent prodding of Jewish students, I now have three examples; this, despite the fact that the Jewish lore in other sections of the archives is unusually well represented, and the Old Testament has a dozen examples of those who return from the dead. Be that as it may, Jewish people in this state seem not to tell stories of this type.

ACTIVITIES

I have made constant suggestions as to the activities of ghosts. By this time the reader must be aware that almost the entire range of human action is represented, except the procreative act and childbirth. The love life of ghosts is exceedingly platonic. Ghosts eat, drink, work, and play with all the diversity of the race. Probably the commonest ghostly activity is walking, indoors and out; the other most frequently represented doings are the pulling of bedclothes off the living, the saying of mass by a priest, the opening and closing of doors and shutters, and riding in an automobile.

As one works over material of this sort he develops a fondness for certain specimens whose ghost life is out of the ordinary. I like particularly the old codger up in Kast Bridge who fussed around the house at dawn every morning until he got into the closet where he had kept his fishing tackle, then sat by the millpond for a while fishing: when he tired of that, he drowned himself again. I like the ghosts who give merry parties and those who sit by the fire and smoke. I like the ingenuity of the heartsick lass, a suicide, who, night after night, came dripping out of the swimming pool, went upstairs to the bedroom where lay asleep her sister and brother-in-law, who was to have been her husband until he changed his mind. Standing by their bed, she tossed her wet hair across their faces, drew it toward her, and departed.

About one revenant in ten speaks to the living, while every third ghost makes one of a wide variety of noises. European stories tend to contain the element of discourse more frequently than American stories. The commonest excuse ghosts have for speaking is to warn the living or to give them information. They give directions — frequently for finding treasure or their own corpses. They call, make requests, offer help, sing, bless, and go through religious ceremonies. It should be noted here that implicit in the story of the vanishing hitchhiker is her conversation with the driver of the car; this is usually short and consists of simple directions to her home, but in the type where the hitchhiker is a nun a somewhat extended conversation is likely to transpire.

Ghosts exhibit more imagination in making noises than they do in conversation. They groan, cry, scream, yell, moan, wail, howl, "holler," and sing; they curse, laugh, whoop, whisper, cough. Perhaps the saddest sound of all is that of the ghosts of babies crying in the night. The groan, cry, and scream are the commonest noises made with the voice, but when it comes to noises made by the hands, feet, or body, footsteps are much commoner still. Some other small classifications are clapping hands, rattling of bones, the sound of a body being dragged or falling — a kind of re-creation of the sounds made at the time of the ghost's death. The traditional rapping of ghosts is an active element in the current stories, as is the clanking of chains, of which I have several examples, one of them Irish. Such noises as hammering, the tinkling of glasses, the rattling of dice, the squeak of a wheelbarrow, the tapping of a ferule on a desk, and carriage wheels are all to be heard, but none of them very frequently. There are other noises which are made by parts of a house, like the banging of doors, window shutters (always on a windless night), the creaking of floors and faint unpleasant noises in the attic. Previous mention has been made of orchestras playing, but besides that the violin, piano, and accordian are heard. Sometimes the instruments are real ones the ghosts borrow, on other occasions they apparently bring their own. There is something especially piquant about a family awakening at night to hear their dead son downstairs playing his violin in his own characteristic manner. Nor are the ghostly animals silent, the hoofbeats of ghostly horses are commonest, but a Texas tale told in New York tells of a horse that screams as he re-enacts his plunge to death; the dogs growl and bark; the cat howls; and a ghostly cow in Greene County moos. Combinations of sounds are not unknown, by any means, but the most interesting phenomenon of sound relates to the ghost train mentioned above which muffles all sound as it passes, and even if a fast freight is highballing down the far track at the same instant, nothing can be heard.

There is a large group of occurrences which the people describe or include in their narratives and believe to be caused by ghosts, or at least supernatural agents, because no other explanation is satisfying to the narrators. Frequently the ghost is neither seen nor heard, but his deeds are discernible and recognized as his by the true believers. A ghost readily gets the credit for an unexplained movement of an inanimate object in a place believed to be haunted. If the phone dials when no one is near it, or a chair rocks, or the bedclothes are pulled off a bed, or the bolt on a door is pulled back, if household articles are mysteriously moved, if a man's hat is knocked off, a clock wound, a cat let into the house when all the doors are locked, or if the scattered bones in a cemetery return without help to their burial places, then, it is reasoned, the dead are moving about in those parts and keeping busy.

There are certain natural events which are explained by ghosts. The darting about a room of a fireball has already been mentioned, and similarly a fire over a grave or a flame which lifts several feet above its candle are believed due to a ghostly presence. The bloodstain which can not be cleaned away is the stock in trade of historic tea shops. The refusal of horses to draw certain corpses, their tendency to buck and rear in the presence of ghosts which they see, but humans do not, goes down as part of their natural sensitiveness to the supernatural.

Some unnatural incidents lead to concrete results: A mysterious light in the dead priest's study shines on a particular book; in it is found money to pay for a mass he had failed to say; a skeleton is found under the woodpile where the ghost told the living it was hidden; in Sicilian buried treasure stories the treasure is occasionally found where the ghost told the living to look; and the address the vanishing hitchhiker gives invariably has some one there who admits that the ghost was once a member of the family.

Probably mention should be made under this general heading of the appearance of the dead in some spot at a distance from their place of death, at about the same time they die. Sometimes they announce their deaths to friends or relatives, at other times the subject doesn't come up at all.

ATTITUDES TOWARD GHOSTS

Up to this point we have been primarily concerned with the ghosts themselves and their activities. Certain other elements of the stories now demand our attention. The stories frequently contain a charm or ritual to lay the ghost or some accident or event after which the ghost never reappears. Eighty percent of these charms are found in the stories of American locale, indicating that this segment of ghost belief has been actively alive together with the other elements of the narrative.

I find five basic groupings into which the devices for laying ghosts fall. *Religious charms* are reported by Catholic informants and include masses, exorcism, crossing oneself (Italian), the use of holy water, and speaking to the ghost "in the name of the Lord." An equal number of narratives involve the use of *violence or rebuff.* A living corpse was drawn into a circle by the family priest and knocked down; that settled him. Others are shot — two by silver bullets, although in one of these instances it was to no avail. An old German who lived on the south side of Dumpling Hill kept by his bed a musket loaded with a verse of scripture. This would be useful in driving away either ghosts or witches. The rebuffs indicate the wisdom of a firm and uncompromising attitude: one is to order the ghost to "leave the house," another is to refuse to do as it wishes. An informant explains carefully that "ghosts won't do you no harm if you ain't afraid of them." And another, "If you ask a ghost three times, 'What dost thou want?' it will go away and not return."

There is a variety of ways to rid a haunted house of its "ha'nt." The two most effective appear to be most drastic: tear the house down or burn it down. The same results have been achieved, however, by making repairs, remodelling, moving the house to a new foundation, or by putting in a new doorsill.

Certain *actions pertaining to the body of the deceased* are sometimes efficacious in putting the dead to rest. Where a leg or arm has been buried apart from the remainder of the body it should be dug up and reburied with the corpse, so that the ghost will not forever seek it. Though there is no clear-cut evidence that modern ghosts insist upon being buried in graveyards, yet they show a disinclination to having their bodies hidden away in wells or under woodpiles, or other unorthodox spots. Reburial in a cemetery satisfies. A strange Russian story tells of digging up the corpse of a very active ghost, cutting the head off the corpse and putting it between his legs and then reburying him. It too sufficed.

For the ghost who has left behind *unfinished business* discernment on the part of his survivors is necessary. Fire, however, is generally a solution to the problem. The burning of his letters, a comb and mirror, old clothes, a crutch satisfied the spirits in some cases. Two Italian ghosts did not reappear after treasure in which they were interested was located. When a Polish woman's debts were paid, and when the mutilator of an Italian woman's corpse was killed each of them was satisfied. A dead Irish woman whose husband was about to remarry came to him greatly disturbed lest her successor fall heir to her shoes. To make peace he had to sprinkle the shoes with holy water and give them to the poor.

I have no statistics and no yardstick by which to measure the attitudes of informants toward this material. There are four classes of ghostlore, and the attitudes toward each vary. The person who tells of his own *personal experience* is almost always certain that he actually was in contact with the dead. These people are not spiritualists, nor necessarily superstitious, but they have had or believe they have had a supernatural experience. Once again, this cuts across all lines of class, education, and origin. Whatever their experience and their reaction to it at the moment, by the time they tell of it, they are confirmed believers. Then there is the story which is a *family tradition*. These are often told as something once believed in, but now doubted or believed in only by some members of the family. Nor is this matter of belief dependent upon age or sex, but rather upon some quality of mind possessed by the individual and often influenced by a feeling of family loyalty. ("If my grandmother said it was so, it was.") *Neighborhood tradition* is handled much more cavalierly and acceptance or disbelief will conform to the general credulity of the narrator. Then there is a fourth category, the *popular ghost tale* of which the hitchhiker is the prime example, although there are hundreds of others current in the United States. Attitudes vary again in the telling of these, but there is a marked tendency to offer them as though they were validated facts. ("My cousin's brother-in-law picked up this girl.") Frequently, of course, these stories are told in middle-class social gatherings, and the attitude of belief is assumed for artistic reasons, but many times it is not just assumed. People will tell you, "Of course, I don't believe in ghosts or any such nonsense, but a funny thing happened to my father, and he swore it was true."

On the surface the people of New York State (and my guess is that they are typical of the country) disbelieve in ghosts, but very frequently we find reservations in their minds as regards one particular incident or story. There is the breach in the fortification of their disbelief.

One more word about the popular ghost tale: it tends to be longer, more dramatic, more filled with detail than the family and neighborhood traditions. Perhaps it is slightly influenced by the literary ghost tale to which it is related. Many of the items in the archives are bare statements of fact, totally lacking in elaboration, but the tales are richer, better constructed as narratives, frequently having strong elements of suspense and surprise. This is partly due to the narrative abilities of informants, some of whom doubtless make much out of little, but it may ultimately be found that there are more important differences. In this connection, I might observe that a disproportionate number of the European items tend to fall into this group.

CONCLUSIONS

Certain general conclusions can be drawn from this study: Ghostlore is still widespread and popular. There is a great range and variety of detail in the stories, some of which is very up to date. While most of the actions thought to be common among ghosts (chain clanking, cemetery haunting, and so forth) can be found, they are by no means so widespread in the popular ghostlore as we have been led to expect. The ghost who is very like the living is far more common than any other. The one universal characteristic of ghosts is the ability to vanish or fade out of sight. Most ghosts are found to be harmless, many of them even helpful. Violent death is frequently a factor in becoming a ghost. The reasons for returning are varied, but most prominent are the completion of unfinished business and a desire to warn or inform the living. The geographic distribution is found to follow New York's two great river valleys, areas which in later years have drawn folk from European cultures where ghostlore is believed. While this latter group have brought, in their European stories, elements not found in the American stories, the differences are of degree rather than of kind.

It might be expected that a rational age of science would destroy belief in the ability of the dead to return. I think it works the other way: in an age of scientific miracles anything seems possible. Especially in wartime, tragically large numbers of the living yearn to see and hear again the dead. If radio controlled planes, robot bombs, penicillin, and radar are to be everyday experiences, then people open their minds to possibilities that are nearer their deepest wishes and hopes. If I may hazard a parting guess, it would be that there will be an increase rather than a decrease in ghostlore during the coming decade.

The Devil in York State

WHILE there are any number of stories about contemporary ghosts, and while the papers occa-occasionally carry accounts of witchcraft in our time, the Devil seems not to come among us any more, at least not in a form we recognize. This is not to belittle the amount of deviltry that is going on in our day and our land, nor is it to ignore the fact that there is always the Devil to pay. What I say is merely that the stories men and women tell of his visits to New York State are old stories—probably the most recent of the events recounted, more than a half century old. There are, of course, stories about the Devil as he appeared in Europe, told by families of recent European origin, and then there are the stories with which I am concerned here, in which the locale is American. As the Devil says to Daniel Webster in Stephen Benèt's great short story, "Who has a better claim to the name 'American'"?

There are a number of place names in New York which commemorate His Satanic Majesty. Up in Warren County between Chestertown and Warrensburg there is a deep gully known as the Devil's Kitchen, and near Elmira there is a treacherous bend in the road known as the Devil's Elbow. The State of New York has named two parks in his honor—the Devil's Hole near Niagara Falls and the one near Phoenicia, known optimistically as the Devil's Tombstone.

Long Island has had its place legends about the Devil, as

C. M. Skinner noted in his *Myths and Legends of Our Land* where he told, as others have told before and since, of how the Devil cleared the island of stones by throwing them across the sound at the Indians who had driven him out of Connecticut. That he stayed on Long Island for some time is evidenced by footprints in many places between the East River and Montauk.

Men have never agreed as to the appearance of Satan, and men have seen him in a multitude of guises through the centuries. Nor do the stories told of him in our land create a single, unified portrait. Rarely, it might be observed, does he appear as the naked, red-skinned, horned and tailed creature of caricature; most frequently he is a smooth and elegant gentleman, his diabolic character betrayed only by the claws within his beautiful gloves, or by the dainty hoofs beneath his striped trouser leg. Pete C., who lived near Highland, said that when he saw the Old Boy, he appeared as "tall, well built, with black hooves, and a bristled tail." That day when he offered to make Pete his right-hand man, he was wearing a "black suit, tied at the ankles, and he had silver chains around him a-clankin' away." It was after that encounter that Pete stopped drinking, and these are the words of a sober man.

Sometimes the Devil is a little man or a black man or an old man; sometimes he comes in animal form, as a horse, a dog, a lamb, a rabbit. Protean is the best adjective to describe him. But we come back, time and again, to that suave, charming, insidious character who entered the popular mind sometime after the Renaissance, that elegant character, Mr. Scratch, the Old Boy.

The Devil has long been appearing among men as a dog; did he not appear thus to Faust and to Pope Silvester II? Well, "they" still tell of his doing it. Set back a bit from the banks of the Poestenkill Creek, not far from Troy, there is a house that is deserted now; but not many years ago it was the scene of a visit from Satan in the form of a big black dog, and the evidences of that visit, they tell me, are still to be seen. It happened this way: a girl was dying in that house, and it was decided that her brother should go to get the parish priest; as the boy left he noticed a black dog going in the house, but he was preoccupied and thought nothing about it. By the time the boy returned with the priest, the dog had found the girl's room and had withstood all efforts to remove him. A few minutes later the priest came hurriedly out of the room and left the house without a word to anyone, but somebody observed that there were long scratches on his neck. As soon as he heard about this, the girl's brother rushed after him. When found, the priest was a badly shaken man; not only had he been physically mauled by the dog, but, far worse, he had been spiritually defeated, for, he explained to the brother, his sister was damned. As soon as the priest had kneeled to pray for the girl, the beast had set upon him and clawed him. He was persuaded to return to the house where they found the sister dead, with red claw marks on her forehead; and burned into the floor by her bed were cloven marks. The family moved away, and the house has long been empty, but on Good Friday the people still see a black dog prowling about the premises.

Sometimes men who put their minds to the task can outwit Mr. Scratch and even, on occasion, set him to useful work. One of the ways is to treat him badly when you have him in your power. From a woman of French Canadian background comes a story of our North Woods where a group of men were building a church. One day a beautiful white horse that none of them had ever seen before appeared from nowhere; it kept getting in their way and bothering them, so that their work was slowed up. Finally they put a harness on him and made him do the heaviest work; soon he proved a great help to them, but when the priest saw what was going on he had some sage advice for them: "Make the horse work as hard as you want to, but give him no food and no water." Well, they worked and the horse worked, and after some hours they saw that the beast was getting hungry and thirsty, but they remembered what the priest had told them, and they kept it working without so much as a rest. Finally one of the crowd who was used to treating his own horses decently could stand the obvious thirst of the horse no longer and brought him to a pail to water; as soon as the animal began to drink he disappeared. It wasn't until the priest returned to explain that he had recognized the creature as the Devil that they understood with what forces they had been dealing.

This is apparently a frequent type in French Canadian folklore, for I have two other accounts from north of the border of the Devil as a horse, helping to build a church, though in both of these versions it was the bridle forming a cross which kept him in the driver's power, and when the bridle was removed the horse vanished.

The compact with the Devil under the terms of which man exchanges his everlasting soul for riches, honor, and power in this world is a folkloristic and artistic commonplace in western culture, possibly owing its origin to the temptation of Christ by Satan when he showed Him the whole world.

Usually the Devil is on the alert to find likely bargainers, but some are impatient and seek him out of their own accord. From a Negro whose family is one of the oldest in Albany comes information as to the way men used to call upon Mr. Scratch when they were anxious to make a Faustian bargain. They took themselves to Chatham Four Corners (now Chatham) and killed a black cat and cooked it. Then they removed the backbone and ate the meat at the stroke of midnight, at the very center of the Four Corners. No sooner was this food devoured than things began to happen: the Devil appeared and the bargain was struck; all the money given that the man wanted (though it turned to horse manure as soon as it was spent) until a certain date, at which time the Devil could be expected to appear as a club-footed man or a big black dog. When he appeared the bargainer would know that the game was up, and he would have to go off with him, forever.

There are other ways known in our area for (literally) raising the Devil. Take Victor Tremper, for example, who lived in Farmer's Mills, not far from Stormville Mountain. There can be no question about his reputation: everyone agreed that he was a bad character, and some believed that he had murdered his wife and thrown her body into a pond near his farmhouse, though he was never brought to trial, and no charges were pressed against him. And then people began to say that he had the power to make the Devil appear whenever he had a mind to.

Well, one rainy afternoon a crowd of the boys were hanging around the general store, looking for some excitement. They got to talking about Victor's power and decided there would never be a better time to prove whether there was any truth in the story. So a group of the hardier souls went sloshing through the rain to the old man's house and asked him point blank how good a friend of his the Devil was. For reply he led them out to his weather-beaten barn where he cautioned them first to absolute silence, then drew a circle in the middle of the floor. In the breathless quiet he spoke some magic words that none of them understood. They waited for a moment or two, and then he appeared, the Old Boy himself, right out of the middle of the floor. Well, Victor had proved his power, but I reckon the boys didn't stay around very long. I reckon they were satisfied with what they saw.

Croghan, up in Lewis County, is a town that can boast two citizens who were able to call up the Devil with a little trying. There was Nick Gort, for one. He wasn't much good, and down at the tavern they got fed up with him one night and kicked him out. He was so mad he went home and got out an old book of black magic that he owned and looked up the part where it told how to call up the Devil — I suppose he had some notion of getting even with the tavern keeper. He read the directions carefully and made his arrangements accordingly; we have to take Nick's word for what happened as he told it later on. Then he said the magic words, the ones he found in the book, and the Devil came popping right out of the stove: bright red, had a long tail, and he kept dancing all over the room with a big pitchfork in his long claws. By this time any ideas of vengeance Nick may have had were routed by his own terror. The only thing he could think of was getting rid of the demon; fortunately he had enough presence of mind to remember that further on in the book there was advice on how to get rid of the Devil, once you had him on your hands. The trouble was, you needed a big fire in the stove to do it. Nick piled the stove full of kindling and lit a match, but no sooner was it lighted than the Devil spit it out. Nick tried and tried again, but his unwanted guest had perfect aim and limitless spittle. It took two boxes of matches before Nick could get that fire lit; after that he said his magic words, and finally he was alone again. But the whole business was too close a call for comfort, and after that Nick let magic and such strictly alone.

The other Croghan character to have dealings with the Devil was known as "Old Griot," who died about 1927. The story goes that he was a wizard and could put the hex on a neighbor's cows as easily as you could sneeze in the pepper pot; everybody remembers how all of Billy Zeller's cows died after Old Griot put a curse on them. Well, it seems the Devil was so pleased with the way Old Griot was making out that he came to him one day with a special offer. If Griot could chop off the head of a live goat with one clean, swift stroke of the axe, then he would be a sort of boss among the witches, the Devil's right-hand man; if he failed, he'd just be the Devil's meanest tool. It was all or nothing. Now a goat is a pretty lively sort of critter, and it takes a good deal of persuasion to make one stay still for any length of time; Old Griot knew that if it moved so much as a few inches he was out of luck. Well, he agreed to try, and the Devil prepared the block and brought out a goat and an axe and stood there, leering. The old man fingered the axe, and tried this stance and that; he tried petting the goat, and he shifted his weight around from one foot to another. But it was too much; he got cold feet and couldn't take the chance. So the Devil just looked at him and laughed, the kind of laugh that says, "Ha, you thought you were some punkin' with your hexin' cows, but when it comes to the big chance, you just aren't the man for it!" And after that Old Griot couldn't even hex a cat, let alone a cow. He'd try and try; he'd say his incantations till he was blue in the face, and that was all the good it did him. He wasn't man enough for the Devil.

Satan finds recruits for hell among three special groups: drinkers, card players, and dancers; and many are the stories that tell of his victories or of their narrow escapes.

Walter Peters had been a hard-drinking man for years when, one night, he was on his way home from Lowville to Crystaldale. He was driving along through the woods, quiet and peaceful-like, when out of the darkness jumped Old Nick himself, right up on the back of the wagon. "Hello, Walter, I've got you now! I've been after you for a long time, but I've got you now!" Well, Walter was just as scared as you would have been, and all he could think of to do was to whip up those horses until they were just about flying over the hills on the

Crystaldale road. It didn't take long to bounce Mr. Satan right off the back, and for a moment Walter breathed easier. But the Devil has done a powerful lot of running since he was thrown out of Paradise, and he was still able to get ahead of the horses and grab hold of their bridle, climbing right up on their necks. Then he crawled back until he could hop onto the wagon. "You got rid of me once, but you won't get rid of me again; I've got you now, my fine fellow." And Walter looked at the Devil's hooves and he looked at his claws, and he looked at the leer in his eyes, and right then and there he vowed that if he got out of that pickle, he'd never take another drink as long as he lived. So he grabbed the whip and as they lurched down the road, it just happened, somehow, that old Mr. Scratch fell off a second time, but the fear of all that was unholy went into the lash of the whip across the horses' flanks, and they drove so fast that this time not even the Devil himself could keep pace with them. When he got to his own yard Walter drove those horses into the old barn and sprinted for the house; he found his wife getting supper.

"Hattie," he said, "I've abused you all my life, but I ain't goin' to do it no more. From here on out, I'm goin' to treat you right!"

"Walter," she replied, "Walter, if you ain't feelin' well, you just go on up to bed, and I'll take care of the horses."

But Walter had outwitted the Devil in more ways than one, for never again did he take another drop of liquor.

There is a sad lack of variety in the stories of the Devil as a card player; they fall into a few easily recognizable patterns: an inveterate card player meets the Devil and never again touches cards, or a cardsharp has a two-handed game with Mr. Scratch, or he sits in on a poker game with various results. Our interest, perforce, comes from the details of these stories and the variations of an easily recognized theme.

I know of one York State gambler who played a little two-handed game with the Devil and lived to tell it. Old Ben V. was known in the West Day section as a sharp character with the cards, and many a neighbor was the poorer man for having played with him. Well, sir, one night Ben was sitting at home alone, an unusual circumstance in itself, when he felt a strange presence in the room. None less than the Devil it was, who said he felt like a few hands of cards and couldn't think of a better partner than Ben. When he asked the Devil what the stakes would be, he was ready for almost any answer but the one he got, namely, that if Ben lost, he would never touch a pack of cards again as long as he lived. Of course, the Devil won, and after that you couldn't get Ben to touch a pack of cards with a ten-foot pole. Many a one heard him mutter in the years that followed that he had no intention of giving the Devil a second chance at him.

Then I must tell you of two card games in which the Devil was outwitted, in the first by agility, in the second by the intervention of a priest who knew his business, which is, of course, outwitting the Devil every day in the week.

The first tale goes back four generations or so, in southern Rensselaer County, where there was a group of cronies who used to get together in a shack out in the woods because they were afraid of their wives, good churchgoing dames, every one of them. One night they were playing a little five-card straight, and John Dell was winning, after a long streak of bad luck. Quite unexpectedly there came a rap on the door, and they found there a quiet-spoken man who made himself right to home, as though he had been there before; and when one of the boys went home early, the stranger asked if he could sit in on the game. Nobody objected, but John Dell ran his thumb around the candle about halfway down and said that when the flame reached that spot he was going home. They cut the stranger into the game, and John's winnings began to melt away until he was digging deep in his pockets. That wasn't all that was making him feel uneasy; the candle wasn't burning down, not so much as a quarter of an inch though they played for an hour or more. And so at last he got up and said he was leaving, and the stranger called him a liar and a cheapskate for not keeping his word, and in a minute they were slugging it out, no holds barred. As they were rolling on the floor, John saw the cloven hoof, and he made one long leap, leaving his coat in the stranger's hand; but he was too busy passing jack rabbits all the way home to miss it.

My favorite story of the Devil at the card table comes

originally from Germany, but has long been told in a good American family by the mother who heard it in her girlhood. There were three men in a little town who had been friends for years and whose greatest pleasure came from playing cards together. One evening as they gathered, one of them said jestingly, "May the Devil take the one of us who breaks up this card game!" Half in jest and half in earnest they all agreed to it as to an oath. After a little while a stranger to the inn came over and kibitzed, then asked to be allowed to join the game; but when one of the players dropped a card and saw the stranger's horse-like hooves, he knew that the Old Boy was right on deck to claim his own when one of them should suggest that the game end. Somehow he passed the word on to the other two and they played and played. Soon the sky was gray and then the sun rose, and still none suggested that they stop. They sent for food and they sent for drink, but they kept dealing the cards. Toward dusk the next day the village priest came to the inn, and the bar keeper, who had all the insight of his craft, took him aside and suggested that the boys at the card game were acting mighty queer; as a matter of fact, he thought that there was something strange about that slick stranger who was playing with them; and they all acted as though they were afraid to quit on account of him.

The old priest wasn't afraid of man nor devil. He went over and asked to be dealt into the game, and the boys were glad to oblige. When it came around to his deal, he just put the cards in his pocket, and because he was not a party to the oath, there was nothing on earth or in hell the Devil could do about it, so he was tricked out of his new recruit. But he was so angry, so burned up, as you might say, that he left two hoofprints seared into the floor. And if a man knew the name of the place, and if it's still standing, I'm sure someone would be glad to show them to you, right there in the middle of the tavern floor.

Of the eight or nine stories in my collection telling of the Devil's visit to a dance, more than half of them come from French Canadians. Indeed, one version is the popular dialect verse, "Rose La Tulipe," and is widely known in Canada.

The French Canadian versions, and I have five of them, are current in the northern part of New York, and sometimes the informants localize the stories somewhere in our North Country, or near Cohoes, where there are many French Canadians. While all bear a striking resemblance to the poem I have mentioned, yet each has motifs which indicate an independent development. The poem, obviously, is a late telling of a popular folk tale. And yet, as often seems to happen, the very publication of the poem has strengthened and encouraged the growth of the popular tale. I have chosen the fullest version from those I have, a version told among the French Canadians of Cohoes. You will notice that the girl's name is the same as that in the poem, though the details differ considerably, the tale being the richer of the two.

There was a girl named Rosa Tulip, and in the town where she lived the priest believed that dancing was a sin and an abomination unto the Lord, and he said so, Sunday after Sunday. But Rosa loved to dance, and nothing could stop her from going to every dance she could get to. One night there was one in a nearby village, and when the music started up Rosa was there. After a while she noticed that a tall, handsome stranger had just come in. He soon asked Rosa to dance with him, and then other dances followed; this charming fellow devoted all of his attention to her. As the evening wore on he begged her to take off the chain she wore with a religious medal on it; in exchange he offered her a ruby necklace which he held before her eyes. Now Rosa admired rubies tremendously, but she had never been without her medal as long as she could remember, and although he was insistent and persuasive, she held firm in her refusal.

About this time Rosa's priest stirred from a deep sleep, awakened by some voice that would not be denied. Without knowing why nor whither, the good man dressed, saddled his horse, and, guided by a hand stronger than his own, rode with all speed to the dance hall in the neighboring village. As he arrived at the door, Rosa's partner with the white gloves was just leading her out the door. One look and the priest knew why he had been sent there. He lifted high his crucifix and blessed the girl; as he did so the stranger disappeared into thin air. The only sign of his presence that night were five livid burns, like the marks of five claws, along Rosa's arm where he had been holding her when the priest began his blessing.

One could cull other stories of the Devil from the memories of the people, some of them fragments, others full-fledged tales, but we have sampled the crop, and nothing very startling is left. One wonders, however, what the Devil means to people in our time, and the answer must be as varied as the answerer. For some he is an old joke, a papier-mâché boogie who scared our ancestors and whose name is little more than an expletive. For others, for many others, the Devil is still an evilly majestic figure with the power to tempt an everlasting soul into the fiery tortures of an everlasting Hell.

Italian Werewolves

J UST as some people are born with the evil eye, so others are
are cursed from birth with a tendency to turn into wolves,
under certain circumstances, and go howling through the
night with slavering jaws. I have a few accounts of the appearance of the werewolf, or *loupgarou*, among the French Canadians who live in northern New York, but for the most part it
is from Italians that the helpful information comes.

A typical story is told by one who heard it from her aunt,
who in turn heard it from her mother-in-law's father, who was
a neighbor of the man of whom this account tells. It was nearly
a hundred years ago in St. Angelo, Italy, that a boy was born on
the very stroke of twelve, Christmas Eve. But there was no re-
joicing in that household, for all present knew that the child
born at the moment in the year sacred to the *Bambino* must
carry always the curse of the wolf. His family reared him gently, and he grew to be a likable fellow; except for a few moments each year he was a perfectly normal person.

It was every Christmas Eve that his spell came over him.
At a quarter to twelve he would start off for the church, but
when he got there he would take off his clothes and leave them
on the steps. He would begin by running up and down the
streets, howling into the night; he could see and feel himself
change: his eyes grew blurry; his arms and hair grew long. All
who knew him locked their doors, for all knew that, against his

73

normal will and unknown to his natural self, he would kill anyone he saw.

On one occasion a friend hid in an empty barrel equipped
with a long stick to which was attached a sharp pin. He hoped
that he would be able to stick the werewolf in the middle of the
forehead sufficiently to draw a little blood, thus curing him of
his malady. But unfortunately the mad animal saw him and
rolled the barrel down a hill into a deep stream, where the man
drowned.

When he married, the man-wolf was perfectly frank with
his wife about the whole matter and gave her careful instructions for her protection on the one night in the year when he
would not be himself. (Werewolves seem to be brought back by
some cruel instinct to their own families.) Once he had left the
house, she was not to go to sleep; she should lock the door
against him and not open it under any circumstances until he
knocked *three* times. For a year or two this apparently worked
out satisfactorily, but one Christmas Eve she fell asleep, waking
with a start to hear her husband's knock. Only half awake, she
thought she had heard three knocks and opened the door to
him. But she was mistaken, and her wolf-husband tore the life
out of her throat.

When the spell had passed, he went to a stream of water
and washed himself; as he did, the hair receded and his body
took on its normal shape. Quietly he returned to the church
steps and put his clothes back on. Then he went home, opening
the door upon the torn and bloody corpse of his well-loved
wife. He could not remember, but he knew. He did then the
only thing he could to put his troubled spirit at peace: he took
his own life.

Variants of this story are most frequently heard among
Italian Americans as they remember the werewolves of the old
country. It is a kind of folk classic, and for that reason it will
bear analysis and comparison.

There is almost unanimous agreement among Italians
who know of the werewolf that he is born on Christmas Eve
and that it is on his birthnight anniversary that he runs wild
through the streets and the woods. Occasionally one will tell

you that those who are born in the full of the moon are liable to this lycanthropy, and that whenever the moon is full and it is midnight, the sickness may come over them. Usually the spell lasts but for a few hours, regardless of when it comes; only one informant insists that it comes three successive nights: Christmas Eve, Christmas night, and the night of Christmas Second Day. Always it is midnight.

There seems to be some indecision about the exact shape which the werewolf takes. In the story just told, it is implied that while his hair grew long, and the inner spirit of the man became lupine, yet he was a man-shape. Very often the metamorphosis is complete: the nails grow into claws, the face becomes a snout, and the body hair turns to fur; he runs on all fours; the man has become a wolf in every respect. Some think of him as "half man, half wolf," but one and all agree to the bright, bloodshot eyes, gleaming through the night.

The attempt to prick the werewolf so that a few drops of blood will fall is the standard procedure for bringing one out of his fit. This need only be a minute scratch, though some insist that he must see the blood. There is disagreement as to the permanency of the cure thus affected; while one will tell you that it brings him out of his spell for that night only, others are most emphatic in insisting that the flowing of his own blood while in his wolf-shape will cure him forever. Obviously it was this hope which caused the friends to make such careful preparations for pricking the werewolf of St. Angelo.

Among the French Canadians this striking of the *loup-garou* must be done with a key, a heavy one, and the drawing of blood is not always considered necessary.

The method used by the werewolf to reassume his own shape, namely, bathing in water, is the traditional one. Sometimes his friends or family threw a bucket of water over him to hasten the process.

While some will tell you that a werewolf never dies, others insist he can be killed by the conventional silver bullet or by pricking *three* times with a needle. The trouble with this last is that it is so hard to get near enough and have time enough to do it. By the time you get to the third prick, the werewolf is gnawing at your throat. Many of the accounts speak of the danger of a werewolf killing those he attacks, and it is evident that he is fatally attracted to members of his own family.

One interesting protective device against a werewolf is to stand on the third step of any stairway, especially on the third step of a church porch. And, of course, no werewolf has any power not implicit in his wolf-shape.

Another story which is frequently repeated among Sicilians and Italians concerns a bride and groom. They were happy together, and whenever an opportunity arose, they would pack a little lunch and have a picnic together in the woods. One day the wife had wrapped a lunch for them in a great white napkin, and they went happily into the forest where they blissfully spread out their food and ate it. After a little while a cloud passed over the husband's spirits, and he said that he was going for a little walk by himself. There were, he told her, wild dogs in those parts and he was insistent that she climb a tree before he went off, so that he would be sure she was out of harm's way. A few minutes after he had left, she heard a noise in the brush and looking down saw a wolf coming toward her with terrific speed. She watched from her perch while he pawed the ground and howled up at her; but she was increasingly afraid and in her fright she dropped the napkin she had thoughtlessly carried up the tree with her. The beast clawed at it and tore it to shreds with his teeth. After a while he went away, and a long time after that the poor, scared girl climbed down. When her husband returned to her he seemed exhausted — too tired even to listen to her terrified recital. Indeed, he went to sleep while she was telling him about it. As he slept his mouth fell open, and to her fresh horror she saw the threads of her white napkin caught between his teeth. Only a few weeks after that the young wife died. An unusual element in this tale is the daytime scene, whereas usually action takes place at night.

It is worth observing that among the French Canadians the werewolf stories have York State locales, though I have no stories from them of outstanding merit. They are, rather, mere assertions that werewolves are to be found in our Adirondack region — nothing to compare with the bloodcurdler Harold W. Thompson tells in *Body, Boots & Britches* (p. 115) in which a dead man returns in the form of a *loup-garou*, one of the best of the many stories in that remarkable volume.

In Europe there are many stories of other shapes which men take besides that of the wolf. One such tale has come to our state from the province of Barre, in northern Italy, of a man who was born on the midnight of Christmas Eve, but who, on occasion, took the form of a pig. When he married, his wife learned that when he was away on his strange missions she must put out by the door a bowl of pig feed and a tub of water. Always he came home, ate the feed, immersed himself in the tub of water, and thus became a man again. When his child was born it was perfectly normal, but the man's wife forbade his seeing it when the pig spells were upon him.

In conclusion it ought to be noted that among the great variety of people living in New York State to whom the werewolf is a folkloristic commonplace in their native lands, it is only with the French Canadians and Italians that the material seems to survive in this country in any profusion; it should also be observed that the French Canadians have given the material an American locale in their narratives, whereas the Italians tell the stories as having happened only in the Old World.

Practitioners of Folk Medicine

T HE practitioner of folk medicine in America goes by many different names, and unfortunately there is no clear-cut classification on which we may rely. The names change from region to region, even from community to community.

The *herb doctor*, the yarb doctor or yarb woman is, generally speaking, one who relies almost entirely upon herbals rather than upon any use of magic or the supernatural. A *healer* is frequently one who combines a knowledge of herbs with a careful use of white magic, that is, magic used for positive and moral purposes as opposed to black magic, used by the Devil's disciples for evil purposes. In New York State the word "healer" is very generally used and seems to have replaced the term *witch doctor* which was common, especially in the German communities, even as late as a generation ago. The witch doctor originally, it would appear, was primarily concerned with the patient who had been bewitched or whose sufferings came from the machinations of a witch. In the Ozark Mountains, according to Vance Randolph in his excellent compilation, *Ozark Superstitions*, the common term is *power doctor*, and the power doctor is often a specialist, just as healers and witch doctors are often specialists in this part of the country. The term, *powwow-doctor*, however, is very common among the Pennsylvania Germans, and once in a while we find the term creeping into the Southern Tier of New York which borders on Pennsylvania. The powwow-doctor, again, is both learned in herbals and folk medicine and in devices for counteracting witchcraft. I notice among those of our people whose traditions are rooted in Ireland that we sometimes hear the term *good man*, not to be confused with the Irish expression "good people" used for the fairies. There are other terms in use, but these I think will be the most commonly found in the United States.

Among all these practitioners, regardless of nomenclature, will be found specialists whose reputations depend upon a bent for special types of medical problems. This is just as true with the folk practitioners as it is with the medical profession itself. There has been, for example, in central New York for three generations, a family of bone-setters; for more than seventy years, all through the area covered by Delaware, Schoharie, Otsego, Madison, and Onondaga counties people have had faith and confidence in their abilities. In the eighties and nineties the grandfather of the present practitioners would go into a town and set up headquarters in a local hotel or saloon, and word would go out that he was there. All those with broken bones, or dislocated shoulders, would line up outside his room, pay him his fee of fifty cents, and take the cure. He was a big powerful man with stubby hands who used only physical methods. Very often the victim would scream with pain, but there are many stories current of the crippled children and adults whom he cured. Tradition even gives him credit for curing sufferers from infantile paralysis.

While in the North we have no *snake-bite doctors* such as are common in the southern mountains, we do have people who are *blood stoppers*. In Natural Bridge, New York, there was in recent time a woman of French and Indian descent who could stop bleeding by repeating certain Indian words. The stories tell, as so often in the folklore of these practitioners, that she was especially successful when the regular physicians failed to bring about the desired results. The folk telling these stories are always delighted when they can say, "Of course, the city doctors don't take any stock in this sort of thing, but when they failed we would go to so-and-so, and she could fix you up." Indeed, much of the reputation of these practitioners rests on the fact that they are given credit for bringing about cures which the medical doctor cannot do.

Another blood stopper was Aunt Nanny Saltsman, one of a famous healing couple in the Mohawk Valley. One family tells that when a child cut its foot badly Aunt Nanny was called in. She gently took hold of the injured foot and gazing off into the distance toward the hills, muttered some phrases in German, which translated into English were: "I conquer this blood in the name of the Father, the Son and the Holy Ghost." No sooner had she said it than the blood ceased to flow. Aunt Nanny and her husband were also specialists in "sweeney," a term the folk used both for the disease of horses and for atrophy of the muscles in humans. The patient had to come to the Saltsman home before daybreak, and neither the patient nor the practitioner dared speak a word before the practitioner began to repeat certain charms in German and to stroke the diseased member three times during each of the three repetitions of a verbal charm. This whole process had to go on three mornings in succession, and it took as many days for the cure to become effective as there were days from the day of the inception of the disorder to that when the patient came to the Saltsman house. My informant says, discussing this cure, "You had to have *belief* in it. If you didn't believe, they couldn't cure anything."

Other specialists, like Black Kate Laurisch, a big, hairy, homely old woman who also lived in the Mohawk Valley, were "*baruchers*" specializing in erysipelas and other skin eruptions. Her methods involved heating an iron shovel in the fire until it was red hot, and then a thread, presumably from the clothing of the patient, was placed on the shovel. When the thread had burned, she waved the shovel over the affected part chanting in an indiscernible mumble certain phrases that she well knew by heart. Very often several treatments were necessary, and it was always important that the patient please Black Kate during the process because she was easily irritated. If she didn't like a patient, she refused to cure him. Black Kate, who died only a few years ago, lived in a community where witchcraft no longer had any followers even in its simplest forms, but the ritual of burning the thread bears evidence of that earlier fear and faith.

The specialist in the removal of warts is to be found in all communities where folk medicine persists. The grandfather of a former student of mine who came to this country from Germany was known in the Utica area as a healer with this special ability. He was a tall, white-haired, peace-loving man, greatly loved and respected in the entire neighborhood. It was well known that he had a certain prayer book, or magic book, which he kept under lock and key. One of the interesting things about Simon Sylvatius is that he spent considerable time praying and fasting for every cure that he made, and it took a great deal out of him. This was not something he did casually but something to which he devoted his whole immortal soul during the process of cure. Cures for warts are, of course, infinite in their variety; Sylvatius touched the wart and prayed over it. And the people remember that the warts went away.

Another type of specialist is the one who can talk the fire out of a burn, and still others specialize in cancer, and in the diseases of children, particularly the removal of thrush from the mouth and the problems of feeding.

I might call attention to the fact that for a long period of time many communities had Indians living by themselves as hermits who knew the Indian herbal and medicinal lore. I remember, as a child growing up in Albany, an Indian basket maker who lived in the outskirts of town to whom people turned for all kinds of medical advice. He made herbals in the spring and peddled them along with his baskets. But particularly I remember a spring tonic which he sold in small brown bottles without a label, which cured all the aches, pains, fevers, and worries of the springtime.

One of the most interesting specialists in folk medicine of whom I know was a German woman who lived not long ago in Syracuse whom we might think of as a diagnostician. She was called a "rag doctor," and her technique was to take a piece of white linen cloth and put it around the diseased part of the body. Then she placed the cloth against her own forehead, removed it, gazed at it, and saw in it not only the name of the disease from which the patient was suffering, but also the remedy which she forthwith made and applied. I am told that the rag doctor was sufficiently successful so that she could send her son to medical school and that today he is a practising physician.

In passing we have mentioned various techniques used, but I would like to discuss and classify the various methods used by the folk practitioners. Of course, a great many of them were conversant with the abundant *herb lore* which has been the property of the human race for thousands of years. Along with the herbals were other kinds of *brew* and *concoction* which, properly made, often with certain rituals involving magic, were believed to be efficacious. A good example of this is a kidney cure used by a grandniece of the famous "Bull" Smith of Putnam County, New York. This woman had a "touch with animals," and she could cause spiders to come down out of their webs and then cause them to go back again. Mice would come out of their holes to take food from her hand. But sometimes she had to kill mice to use them in curing kidney trouble. She would skin the mouse, boil it and feed the hind legs to sufferers from those disorders. When a child had a fever and the doctors couldn't cure him she would kill a chicken, slit it open, and while it was still warm she would stick the child's feet in it and this would "draw out" the fever. As our informant said, "Them doctors don't like to admit nuthin' like that, but they had to admit she cured 'em."

But herbals and brews aren't always necessary. Sometimes the *power of the word* is sufficient, and an old witch doctor who lived in the Canajoharie, New York, area would straddle the bed of a sick child and following verbal formulae would talk away the sickness. Others would accomplish this, not with formulae but with *special prayers*, and when you find the folk doctor who follows the technique of prayer you almost always have a consistently devout person, though not always a churchgoer.

I have already mentioned the fact that some practitioners use heated objects in various ways and that originally this was to drive the witchcraft out of the patient. The *laying on of hands* is, of course, tremendously important, and it is most important with the godly type of healer. Sometimes a certain kind of grease was used, or unguent, a "white unguent" as distinct from the "black unguent" used by witches to make it possible for them to fly through the air. The use of greases, particularly goose grease and skunk oil, spread on the hands of the healer and used as kind of a massage was by no means uncommon. But even here the important thing was the hand itself. As one such woman said, "The power of the Holy Ghost has inspired my hands to do this work." And witnesses tell how this same woman, coming to a feverish patient, thrashing about in his bed, would lay her hands upon him, and he would become calm, and his breathing would grow regular, and the cure would begin from that point forward.

The use of magic for medical cures is by no means unknown. Especially in Pennsylvania we get reports of the powwow-doctors drawing a magic circle around the house in which the patient lay and another around the bed of the patient and then sometimes describing a circle around the injured or diseased part. Gradually by incantation and the use of various kinds of verbal formulae they drove the evil spirit out from within these circles. This calls to mind that in most of these techniques we are dealing with matters that are often far older than Christianity, going back to Egyptian and Phoenician civilizations. The insistence on having the full name of the patient, his date of birth, and the ability often to cure *in absentia* by the exertion of great willpower on the part of the practitioner, all point to the devices of the magicians of the twelfth, thirteenth and the sixteenth and seventeenth centuries.

Over and over again, too, we find reference to the use by the practitioners of a "special" or "secret" book. Who wrote these books and what was in them? Certainly we do not have knowledge in all cases, but certain volumes we know to have been and still to be very common and typical. I would like to speak of two of them particularly, the work of Albertus Magnus, published under a variety of titles including, as in my own edition, *The Egyptian Secrets or Black and White Art for Man and Beast, revealing the forbidden knowledge and mysteries of the ancient philosophers*, and the work of John George Hohman, *Pow Wows, or the Long Lost Friend*. Albertus Magnus, born some time around 1200 and dying in 1280, known otherwise as Albert of Cologne, the Bishop of Ratisbon, and canonized in 1932, was one of the great scholars of the thirteenth century, a contemporary of Roger Bacon, a teacher and defender of Thomas Aquinas. He was the great Aristotelian scholar of his time, interested in and learned in geography, astronomy, zoology, botany, alchemy, and especially in medicine and natural magic. By natural magic, of course, he meant good magic,

magic to be found in Arabic writings along with information regarding the virtues in herbs and stones.

Albertus Magnus probably did not write the work that carries his name, but it is significant, I think, that one of the great scholars in magic and occult studies should have his name attached to this collection which has been so widespread and so generally used and held in such high esteem. A few excerpts will show you what type of material it contains and the character of its cures and charms. While this was probably only one of many books which circulated even as late as the twentieth century in America among folk practitioners, it is the most famous and most potent of them. It was to these folk practitioners what the work of Osler, Cushing, and Welch are among medical men today. There is no way of knowing how many editions of this book have been printed or in how many different languages, nor with how many differing texts, but it is always in print in our own time, usually appearing in little paper bound editions.

There is a considerable variety of information in the work of Albertus Magnus. First of all, there are *cures* for both internal and external medical disorders. Take for example the cure for "a youth contracting hernia or rupture." "Cut three bunches of hair from the crown of the head, tie it in a clean cloth, carry it noiselessly to another part of the county, and bury it under a young willow tree so that it may grow together therewith. This is a sure remedy." When a person "cannot pass water, take black carroway [*sic*] seed, like grains of incense, of each one ounce, lay upon live coals and inhale the fumes. It's a well confirmed remedy." "For epilepsy, purchase a half-grown black rooster, capon the fowl, take a nutmeg and put it in the place from which you made the cut, leave the nutmeg in this place until the rooster is fat, then kill the fowl, withdrawing the nutmeg and scrape, evenings and mornings, the part of a knifeful and add it to a spoonful of soup which is given to the patient. Furthermore, the baptismal name of the afflicted person must be written six times upon a piece of paper and laid under the head of a corpse. Furthermore, perspire in a linen cloth and wrap it around a dead person. If it is a female who has this disease add the powder made by burning to a crisp a lock of her hair. In the case of a male person, leech him and dip a rag into the blood and let it be buried with the corpse. This remedy probat." — These are two typical cures — two of many.

Obstetricians may find Albertus useful to insure a nearly painless and safe childbirth when the natural pains are at hand. "Take a handful of white mugwort or artemesia, a similar quantity of maletha, four ounces of lavender flowers (all these herbs must be dried), four ounces of galligan, four ounces cinnamon, two ounces fennel seed. All these cut fine and pound them, afterward two ounces of wine poured over them and boiled down over a quick fire. Then strain through a cloth and quickly give to the patient to drink. Sweeten the beverage either with honey or sugar. If the child is a stillborn child add to the above drink a handful of senna and another of southern tree."

We might turn briefly to the *veterinary information*, which is also found in Albertus Magnus. Much of this information concerns the care and treatment of cows, which were the most likely victims of the machinations of the witches. "First of all, to cause the cow to give a good supply of milk, you take during Christmas night the meat of a herring and the sinews thereof, also bay leaves, saffron, black carroway seed and mix together, and give it to the cow." "To restore the usefulness of a cow, write the words given below upon three scraps of paper, nail one on the outside of the stable door, the other on the manger and the third tie to the left horn of the cow and speak:

Byan, punctum, sobat,
Byan, punctum, sobat.

This should be repeated three times and then one says, 'This assault and trouble shall cause thee no more pain as it be to our dear Lord in Heaven and all his disciples as little as God the Father, as little as God the Son, as little as God the Holy Ghost' and this, too, should be repeated thrice."

There are also, in Albertus Magnus, besides veterinary medicine, a number of protective charms against witchcraft, against fire, calamity, death, and particularly interesting charms for spellbinding, that is, for making thieves immobile once they have committed an offense against you. There are charms against rodents and against insects, and there is, as one would expect, a charm for the restoration of manhood — one which employs no hormones: "You buy a pike as they are sold in the fish market, carry noiselessly to a running water, there let whale oil run into the snout of the fish, pour the fish into the running water, and then walk stream upward and you will recover your strength and former powers." There are other rituals for proving someone a witch and for driving out evil spirits. Besides these somber and serious matters there are such useful domestic hints as how to glue glass together. Albertus Magnus' volume, then, is a kind of hodgepodge of magic, folk medicine, herb lore, and household hints, but he was regarded with awe, and the instructions he gives for the spelling of charms, the necessity of calling upon the name of God, the importance of saying each formula three times — all of this was a matter of great secrecy and great importance. I want to emphasize this about the book of Albertus Magnus — that it is entirely white magic — there is no maleficium here — this is wisdom to be used to the benefit of man and beast, and it brings harm to none except to witches and thieves against whom it may be used. On the other hand, it may have been possible, by inversions and misconstructions of the text, to produce black magic.

John George Hohman's *Pow Wows, or the Long Lost Friend*, (Edited and published by Aurand A. Monroe, 1922) has probably been as well known and as widely used, especially in German communities, in this country as Albertus Magnus. Hohman's work which was first published in America in 1820, in German, (indeed, not translated into English until 1855) is a compilation of German medical folklore and magic, much of it based upon Albertus and much like Albertus in the type of material it covers. One of the things that has always interested me about Hohman's book is that the book itself is a talisman and a charm. For the first page says: "Whoever carries this book with him is safe from all his enemies, visible or invisible, and whoever has this book with him cannot die without the Holy corpse of Jesus Christ, nor drown in any water, nor burn up in any fire, nor can any unjust sentence be passed upon him, so help me." Hohman's book came into great prominence in 1929 when

a feeble-minded boy named John Blymyer in York County,
Pennsylvania, set out to destroy the power of a witch in his area
named Nelson D. Rehmeyer who he had been convinced had
hexed him. A witch whom he had consulted had advised him
that he must either get a lock of Rehmeyer's hair or his copy of
The Long Lost Friend so that the hex could be removed. Unfortunately, in trying to bring this about, Rehmeyer was murdered
through the undue enthusiasm on the part of young Blymyer,
and the whole matter came into the courts during the trial. The
book continues to sell very widely and continuously, and I am
quite certain that not all of the people who buy it are interested
in it wholly from an antiquarian and folkloristic point of view.

From what has been said already, it must be evident that
across the whole study of folk medicine falls the shadow of
black witchcraft. Certainly the emphasis in Albertus Magnus
and in Hohman makes unquestionably clear the basic fact that
folk medicine grew up in a world in which witchcraft was a tremendously important factor — a society in which everyone, at
all levels, believed in witchcraft and accepted it, considering it
to be as valid as Holy Writ. Nor is it safe to think that the belief
in witchcraft died when the persecution of witches ceased. As
recently as 1930 there was a witch with a good deal of power
operating in the Rensselaer County hills in New York State, and
as recently as 1946 a woman was murdered in Geneseo, New
York, because she had bewitched the man who was to murder
her. Certainly in New York City, throughout the South, and
throughout the West Indies there is abundant evidence easily
available of the continuing potency of the belief in black magic.

Now the folk practitioner had to be able to counteract all
those elements of human disease and animal disease that derived from the curses and plottings of a black witch. If he could
not handle the ailments that were brought on by witchcraft,
then he could not keep his standing in a community that believed in the power of witchcraft. When a community believes
in witchcraft, it tends to lay before its door all the disaffections,
evils, ailments, and tragedies which are otherwise inexplicable.
The necessity for the folk practitioner to understand the coun-
teraction of witchcraft is much like the necessity for the modern
doctor to understand the pscyhological problems of his pa-

tients. The practitioner of folk medicine must know how to counteract black magic with white magic, how to outwit the witch and how, in the name of the Father, Son and Holy Ghost, to cancel out the vile and evil corruptions of the flesh which the black-heartedness of the Devil has perpetrated. The amount of magic used by the witch doctor or healer will be in direct proportion to the prevalence of the belief in black witchcraft in his time and area.

I would like now to consider briefly the calibre of the men and women who were engaged in practicing folk medicine. There is no question, naturally, that a good many of them were just local fakers and frauds. But many of them stand out in the memory of the people as devout, devoted, selfless, and high principled. It is really amazing how sometimes two generations after these healers are dead and gone the memory of them as people of distinguished character and principle remains impressed on the folk mind.

Many of them earned their living by farming or by some craft or trade and would accept no money for their cures. They considered their curing power as the result of a special gift from God, and they felt that any attempt to commercialize it in any way or to make a living from it would cause that special power to be taken away from them. Over and over again we have evidence that the really important healers refused to accept any money for their cures. Some of them did accept gifts, and those who worked without any supernatural aids, like the bone-setters I mentioned earlier, charged a regular fee just the way a doctor would. But among those who utilized white magic, or those who utilized prayer as devices for curing, there was a strong tendency to feel that the accepting of money would destroy their power. Frequently these secrets and formulae which had been traditional in their families could only be transmitted to one of the opposite sex. A man could tell his daughter, a mother could tell her son, but the father could not tell the son, and the mother could not tell the daughter. With some there was the belief that when the secrets of the power had been transmitted for the third time, the individual lost his own power. I remember, for example, one old man who was saving his secrets for his granddaughter because he had twice taught

his cures to other women in the family, and he was waiting until the child was old enough to receive his learning, and then he
felt that his power would be gone. Interestingly enough,
though a great many of the healers were devout and religious
people, very few of them were churchgoers and, in one or two
instances, the special power, which rested in the hands, left the
practitioner when he became engrossed in the church. Certain
persons by birth are especially qualified as healers: the seventh
son of a seventh son and men and women born with a caul over
their faces — which gave them special insight as well as a capacity for divining the future — were considered equally well endowed for becoming healers.

I learned something of the almost saintly regard with
which a community can remember these healers when I was
first doing folklore field work in the Rensselaer County hills in
the 1930s. There was in the area known as Berlin Mountain up
near the town of Tabortown in the period from 1890 to 1915 a
couple named Mr. and Mrs. Franz Engwer, both of whom were
beloved and admired for their unselfish willingness to cure both
man and beast when trouble came. The Engwers had twenty-
eight children, twenty-six of whom stood by their parents'
graves when the time came for them to pass on. My friends,
Lewis Palmer and his wife, who were herb collectors, remembered them with great clarity and spoke of the blameless and
devoted lives that the Engwers lived. Franz Engwer was gifted
in the curing of sick cattle. Palmer told me of one time when
their cow was sick: "her hair stood up and she wouldn't number
one or wouldn't number two, she wouldn't eat and she
wouldn't drink. What little milk she gave was bloody." The
first thing Palmer did was to tap her horn and find that it was
hollow. He bored a hole with a gimlet and filled the hole with
pepper and vinegar, but that didn't do any good. And so he
went over to Engwer's farm and asked him to come. He said
he'd be there late, after dark; they were all to be in bed, and he
was to be left alone with the cow. After the moon came up they
could hear him drive into the driveway, and Palmer, whose
bedroom was at the back of the house, only about ten feet from
the barn door, was interested in knowing how the master healer
worked. He got out of bed and knelt by the open window in the

dark, watching and listening. Engwer opened all the barn doors, went into the barn and began talking to the cow, and finally by the light of the lantern that was there Palmer could see him rubbing his strong, knotty hands along the beast's flank. It was, he reported, a long charm that Engwer spoke with many words, mentioning the Holy Trinity repeatedly. Finally, Engwer said, "Evil, come out of this cow," and those were really the only distinguishable words that Palmer could repeat, but he could see this man whose hands had been working gradually backward down the flanks of the beast pulling gently and slowly the length of her tail. "Evil," he said again, "come out of this cow." Palmer, who had kept himself carefully hidden all this time, then saw Engwer close the barn door, look up into the darkened window where Palmer was hiding, and heard him say, "There, Palmer, she'll be all right in the morning." And, as is always true with these stories, the beast was well.

Mrs. Palmer remembered Mrs. Engwer coming to cure the children of yellow jaundice. She insisted that all the doors and windows of the house be opened, and that everyone in the house be perfectly silent. She read aloud from "her book" in German, and Mrs. Palmer, who was German herself, said "It was all good words like was in the Bible, but I didn't understand it." She made signs of the cross over the child, and she gave in this ritual the child's name and date of birth, and Mrs. Palmer said, "there was parts where the words all had to be said backwards." I remember very clearly Mrs. Palmer sitting by her stove in the kitchen as she talked to me and after a long silence, when we had been discussing the Engwers, she said, "Well, I wisht they was alive today. They'd know what to do about my sky-attic rheumatism. These dumfool doctors today don't know nuttin.'"

In my state certainly the most famous, and perhaps the greatest of the witch doctors was Doctor Jake Brink, about whom Emelyn Gardner has written most capably and most interestingly in her *Folklore from the Schoharie Hills*. Jake Brink, who died in 1879 and is still remembered in the Schoharie and Ulster country, was a specialist in the problems of medicine which were the result of bewitching and was popularly called a "witch doctor." He was of Dutch stock; his grandfather, another Jacob Brink, was the most famous witch doctor of *his* day. A prominent feature of the elder Brink's treatment was a salve, consisting of seven ingredients, of which he had dreamed for three successive nights. It appeared to have wonderful curative properties, and so folks from far and near went to his home to stay and be healed. The younger Doctor Brink inherited this formula and added to his credit a white salve and a famous ointment. His son, from whom Miss Gardner collected valuable information in 1914, told, and others corroborate, that much of his power was in the middle finger of his right hand. It was with this finger, smeared with pottle, that the doctor would describe a magic circle over the afflicted part of the patient, then he was heard to speak strange and unintelligible words in a tongue which men did not understand. Very often he kept three candles burning by the sick bed, and one of the features of his treatment was the silence which he insisted upon enforcing upon all members of the household while he was treating the patient. Doctor Brink, like so many other witch doctors, had a book of magic, and his son remembered seeing the scattered leaves of that book in the attic after his father's death.

Brink's great reputation was made in driving the Devil out of those who had been bewitched. He was called often for children who were suffering in this way, and sometimes he would take the blanket from the child's bed, fill it full of pins, and then with a magic gesture and verbal ritual, he would drive the spirit of the witch out from the child's person. At other times he would steal, or have stolen, an article of clothing from the woman whom he believed to be the witch, and would beat it and beat it with a rod or wand until she came to heel and withdrew her curse from the afflicted one.

A story of this sort is told in the Woodstock area, just outside of Kingston, in the little town of Willow where Beck De-Mille was the most dangerous of the local witches. One day she went to visit Aunt Malindy and was treated pretty coolly, and that night Malindy's beautiful eighteen year old daughter became ill. For weeks her illness came on every night at sunset and lasted until cockcrow in the morning. And in the morning they would find the print of a bit in her mouth, where Beck De-Mille had driven her as a horse through the night skies. The poor girl grew increasingly distracted and lost weight; when she became run down with fatigue Doctor Brink was finally called in. He was told the history of the case; he considered it carefully and finally said, "As soon as I leave, Beck DeMille will come riding up to your door on her big black horse. She will make three requests. Grant none of them because any one of them will give her possession of your daughter." And sure enough, a few minutes later Beck DeMille did ride up, and Aunt Malindy and her husband met her at the door. It was just getting dusk. "Give me that ribbon," designating a bow which the daughter wore. Nobody moved. "Give me that cloak," she demanded next, pointing to a garment which she knew belonged to the daughter. Still no one budged. And then came the third request, "Give me that riding whip." It was the whip the daughter herself used when riding. "I'll give you the whip," the girl's father replied, and with that he snatched it up and gave the big black stallion a terrific lash across the flank. The horse tore out of the yard with his witch rider shrieking her curses, but that night the daughter wasn't ill for the first time in months, and after that Beck DeMille always walked with a limp. She said she had a hip injury. "I slipped on a butternut," she said, if anyone asked her. But the people in the community knew that the horse was her familiar with whose body she could at will exchange spirits.

It is easy enough, in our greater knowledge of science, to make fun both of these men and women who practiced medicine in these terms and of the people who believed in them. But it is, it seems to me, more important that we understand the background from which such beliefs came and appreciate the fact that many of these practitioners were devoted spirits who gave unselfishly of their very best energies and thought to bring relief and to alleviate the suffering of those who were ill. One must in all fairness give credit to many of them for a willingness to serve as physicians in the noblest sense of that word. Their day has past, and they are but a footnote in the history of American medicine but a footnote which it is important for us not to neglect completely.

Murders

THIS section spans my writing career, for "The Berlin Murder Case" was my first significant published article, appearing in *New York History* in April 1936. On the other hand, "Rulloff, The Learned Ruffian" was written in 1980 and has not been previously published. Between those dates I have studied a fair number of murders, always learning about life "below the level of historical scrutiny," as Lyman Butterfield once put it.

The Green case, for example, gives us a wonderful view of small village life, the men sitting around the stove of the general store, the women caring for Mary Ann, the gossip, the social stratifications. "Rulloff, The Learned Ruffian," on the other hand, is a study of a remarkable mind in a man totally lacking in moral sense. It is also a close-up of the life of petty criminals in mid-nineteenth-century New York.

James Taylor Dunn with whom I share responsibilty for "Crazy Bill Had a Down Look" (*American Heritage*, August/ September 1955) was librarian at NYSHA in the fifties and was the one who discovered the Mastin paintings and did the early research on the whole group of thirteen. Freeman's story faces that difficult problem that still plagues us, the culpability of the insane. It is also a sharply focused view of the life of Blacks in the North long after slavery was abolished here, summed up by Freeman's brother-in-law, John DePuy. How much the violent reaction was due to race and how much to fear of a rogue killer is hard to discern at this distance.

Most of the bibliographies for these three cases can be found in Thomas McDade's *The Annals of Murder, A Bibliography:* Green, #384–89; Freeman, #324–25; Rulloff, #835–41.

Diana Trilling, in *Mrs. Harris* quotes the historian, Frederick Maitland, "If some fairy gave me the powers of seeing a scene of one and the same kind in every age of history, in every race, ... I would choose . . . . a trial for murder, because . . . it would give me so many hints as to a multitude of matters of the first importance."

The Berlin Murder Case

THE American people have always been interested in crime news and murder trials. We think of this as a recent development in our national character, but anyone who has read our early newspapers, or who is familiar with the popular murder ballads and broadsides, knows that interest in homicide has long been a part of our folkways. A case in point is the tremendous popular excitement aroused when, in 1845, Mary Ann Wyatt Green, a temperance player, was murdered by her bridegroom of a week, the well-to-do Henry G. Green.

This murder has left a considerable literature behind it. The complete testimony of the trial, the confession of Green published after his execution, the long columns in the contemporary dailies, a poem published with the testimony, a broadside of twenty-four stanzas, and ballads still sung in Vermont attest, ninety years later, to the public interest of the time.

The scene of this tragedy is Berlin, Rensselaer County, a beautiful little mountain village of some 300 inhabitants, about twenty miles from Albany, and about five from the Massachusetts line. The family of Henry Green had been substantial citizens of this community for several generations. Henry's father was dead; his mother, Mrs. Sally Green, and a sister, Mrs. Crandall, lived sixteen miles away in Troy; his brother had married in the village.

Henry was born in 1823; this made him twenty-two in

1845. He started working at the age of sixteen or eighteen as a clerk in Troy. Just when he returned to Berlin and opened his own store we do not know, but it was about 1842, and it was about that time too that he was publicly reprimanded and expelled from the Baptist Church for intoxication. In the summer or fall of 1844, a few months before his marriage, there was a suspicious fire in the store he owned in Berlin. The insurance people settled for the loss, but it was noted laconically at the trial that Henry's uncle, Joel Mallory, was a director of the insurance company.

The most picturesque of Green's escapades was his participation in an antirent riot in October 1844. Disguised as Indians, he and eleven followers freed a fellow townsman, Schuyler Jones, from constable John J. Nichols, who was taking him to Troy for trial. The case was eventually settled; Jones paid his rent, and our friend Green paid a $125 fine. However, participation in such an affair would weigh against him far less in a strong antirent section like Berlin than it would in Troy, the county seat.

We should also notice that at this time Henry had a strong attachment for a young woman named Alzina Godfrey. At the trial Porter Dennison, one of Green's two best friends (the other was Alson Niles), testified that the intimacy between Henry and Alzina had continued all through the summer of 1844. He further stated that Josiah Godfrey, Alzina's father, was "considered a man of large property."

In 1845 Mary Ann Wyatt was twenty-two, the same age as Henry Green. There can be no question but that "she was not of high degree," as the ballad says. Her native hearth was in Thornton, New Hampshire, where she was one of a family of eight children. At the age of eighteen she left home with her brother David to work three years in the mills at Lowell, Mass. Sometime late in 1843 or early in 1844, Mary Ann and David Wyatt joined a traveling company of temperance players, presenting *The Reformed Drunkard*. This may have been a pirated version of P. T. Barnum's *The Drunkard*, which had appeared first in 1843.

In late November or early December they played in Washington Market, Troy. On December 30, they opened a three-night run in Berlin. Mary Ann was observed by the villagers, observed and approved. The next stop of the company was Hancock, across the Massachusetts border. Two Berlin men, Palmer and Crandall, joined them there; then to Lebanon Springs. It was here that Mary Ann and Henry first met, though Green had undoubtedly seen her in Berlin. The next stand was New Lebanon, where Green and a Berlin man named Lyman Bennet joined the company. At first Henry merely sang, but soon he had a part in the play.

Early February found the company in Kinderhook. Whether it disbanded there, or whether the principals of this story merely left the company, I do not know. The intimacy between Mary Ann and Henry had been ripening under the observing eye of brother David since the young storekeeper had turned actor. Mary Ann took her brother's arm less often than had been her wont, turning more and more frequently to Henry for that service. It was with no surprise, then, that David heard Mary Ann ask his opinion of her engagement — his opinion and his consent, which he gave.

On February 5 or 6 (Wednesday or Thursday), Mary Ann and David Wyatt, Henry Green, and Lyman Bennet arrived back in Stephentown, where they had previously given their play. Green and David seem to have left Mary Ann there and gone on to Berlin. Henry busied himself with preparations for his coming marriage which was fixed for Sunday, February 17, a week and more away. On Friday, the eighth, he invited a number of his friends to attend the wedding. These included Alson G. Niles and Porter G. Dennison, Alzina and Mary Rhodes (possibly the daughters of Docter Rhodes, Green's family physician), and Alzina Godfrey, his former sweetheart.

Sunday, February 10, Green left Berlin for Stephentown to see his bride-to-be. Unexpectedly and without explanation, Mary Ann Wyatt and Henry G. Green became man and wife that same day, a full week before they planned. David Wyatt was a witness to the wedding performed by Elder Spoon in the Christian Chapel.

On Tuesday, February 12, the bride and groom, with David Wyatt, left Stephentown, where they had remained after the wedding, and came to Berlin. David went to the home of Lyman Bennet, the man who had been in their theatrical company. The Greens went to a tavern, only to move the next day to the residence of Mr. and Mrs. Ferdinand Hull, at whose home Mary Ann had stayed when she came to the village as a player. Mary Ann was in perfect health at this time.

On the morning of Wednesday, February 13, the third day after the wedding, there came to Berlin from Troy Mrs. Green, Henry's mother, and Mrs. Crandall, his sister. Sally Green did not meet her new daughter-in-law, but established herself in the tavern of Dennison and Streeter (now the Colonial Inn), diagonally across the road from the Ferdinand Hull home (now the Manchester Market), where the newlyweds were staying. She sent for Henry to come to her in the parlor of the tavern.

At the keyhole of the door between the parlor and dining-room there was pressed the attentive ear of Polly Ann Boone, maid of all work for Dennison and Streeter. At the trial she was to testify that the tone of the voices within the room was so restrained that she had to listen quite attentively to gather what little she did. Her largest tidbit from the conversation was Sally Green's statement to her son that she had heard what Mary Ann's character had been when she was in Troy. This referred to the four-day engagement of *The Reformed Drunkard* in Troy, December 1844. Apparently Henry's answer was that he believed his wife to have been and to be virtuous, that he married her for love. Later that afternoon, after his mother and sister had gone, he repeated these sentiments to his friend Niles, adding that he had a wife that suited him, that he had married her for love, that in comparison with the disposition of his recent ladylove, Alzina Godfrey, his wife's was by far the better. Green also told Niles that his mother was going to meet a note of his at the bank; but Niles said at the trial that he could not remember what Green had said regarding his mother's opinion of the marriage. Whatever that opinion was, Sally Green did not cross the street to meet Henry's bride.

After the death of Mary Ann, and Henry's arrest, Mrs. Green wrote her son a letter which corroborates Polly Boone's testimony.

Troy Feb'y 20th 1845

Deare son

It is with the greates anxiety that I wright to you. At this
time I feel to morne with you at this time If weeping wold
doo enny goo[d] but my head has been sow hot that I cant
shead a tear to day I am all most distracted that thay will
prove you gilty If that should be the case I am ondo[ne] and
sow are you and all the rest of the family Henry tell me you
are inisont and dont deceive mee Henry I have binn sorree
that I told you the reports that I hird that I cud weap night
and day I did rong in telling you them at all As I did not
think that it wold make you dislike your wife at all As you
told mee you love hir and mared hir for love If sow how
cold you wish to do sow very rong If you had been deceive
in enny way you cold have left her in a onerable way you
told mee shee was a virtus girl and I believe you and I have
binn sorry th I told you enny hear say reports Aas I dont
believe them at all If this should be the caus of enny that
has Hepen I shall weape night and day as I did not wish to
make you on happy at all Will you for give me and will god
for give mee O i aske it In solem prare to night as the case
will soon be desided be carefull what you say and doo for
youre life depends on it I want to see you very much Indead
right to me once and lett mee now the hool matter as it is as
soon As git this without delay do it Let now on [no one] see
this on now account I remain your sincier frind and mother
till deth mee part good by till we meat agan

Sally Green

Henry G. Green

Apparently it was in compensation for the wedding they
had missed that Henry organized a sleighride for his disap-
pointed guests the day following his mother's visit. They were
his young friends of the town: Anson Niles, Porter Dennison,
Alzina Rhodes, Mary Ann's brother David, and — Alzina Godfrey. It is difficult to determine the actual relations between Alzina and Henry. The Saturday before his marriage, he told
Niles that he supposed Alzina expected, or had expected, they
would marry. This is hardly the statement of a rejected suitor;
yet renewed hope in Henry's mind or an unfavorable compari-

son of his wife and Alzina are about the only explanations which will fit into the facts which follow.

The party left Berlin about noon, heading north down the Little Hoosick River until they came to Hoosick, where they visited the home of Caroline Groesbeck. On the way there happened a little incident of some considerable portent to those involved. All we know of it is that Alzina Godfrey said or did something to make Green regret his marriage. Whatever it was, with whatever intent, it was potent enough to change Henry Green from a happy and contented bridegroom to a headstrong murderer. Rumor declares that Alzina jokingly said she had expected she was going to marry Henry, and that he took this jest seriously, felt he still had a chance with her. It seems more likely that, after some months of absence from Berlin and Alzina, her previous attraction for him in all its ramifications, physical, financial, social, stood out in vivid contrast to the poor, pretty little waif to whom he found himself married after an acquaintance of less than a month. It also clarifies the picture a bit to know that Alzina was considered "something of a highflier."

Mary Ann was slightly indisposed on Thursday; consequently she was susceptible to the cold on the ride to Hoosick. Her brother heard her comment on how cold she was and saw her drink a cup of ginger tea with her hostess. The party returned to Berlin about ten o'clock on Thursday night.

The first move Henry made on Friday morning was to visit his old family physician, Doctor Rhodes. After some genial chat and congratulations to the bridegroom, Green left with some physic pills for Mary Ann who was still slightly indisposed. Though it was not disclosed until his confession, he then procured some opium pills, which he made to resemble the pills he had from Doctor Rhodes. He thought these would kill his wife, but she merely vomited them. More effective measures had to be found.

It was on Friday afternoon that Green dropped into Dennison and Streeter's tavern. The group of men around the bar gave him the jests which are the bridegroom's due, but Henry seemed serious. After a bit he stood at the bar with old Daniel Green, magistrate and schoolmaster. In an offhand way he said that he had been putting some arsenic about his store (which had been closed up since the fire) to get rid of the rats and mice. He wondered how much it would take to kill a person. William Sheldon, another schoolmaster, said he understood you could hold enough on the point of a knife to kill anyone. They failed to tell him that too much arsenic merely delays the death of the victim. Sometime that same afternoon he slipped behind the counter and took arsenic powders wrapped in papers from Dennison and Streeter's store. The custom of self-service in the village made this easy.

It can serve little purpose to recite in detail the story of the next two days. Green seemed very attentive to his wife; he hovered over her bedside constantly; repeatedly he administered liquids in which were white powders at a time when the physician prescribed no liquids. Small quantities of undissolved white powder were found in the crust-coffee, on the spoon which had been in the chicken broth, in nearly everything liquid which Henry administered to his wife. Unknown to Henry, one of the papers with a bit of powder in it was picked up by Mrs. Ferdinand Hull. In the meantime, Dr. Emerson Hull, who had been called on Saturday, was beginning to despair. He called in another physician for consultation. Hull urged that her stomach be rinsed with hot water; her husband objected to this treatment, claiming that she had already vomited too much; he obstructed every treatment for poison which the doctors ordered. There seems to have been a steady stream of solicitous and helpful callers to spell each other in caring for Mary Ann. This continuous file of amateur nurses was a handicap to Henry, for the sharp eyes of these women let little pass unnoticed.

Saturday night and Sunday showed Mary Ann gradually sinking. Twice on Saturday night the neighbor who spelled Henry in watching at the bedside observed him include white powders in his wife's nourishment.

On Sunday afternoon David Wyatt took Doctor Hull downstairs to ask his frank opinion of his sister's chances for life. Hull did not think she could live through the night and that she should be told. David went back to her bedside. She asked him if the doctors had given up hope; then he said to her, "Mary, the doctor thinks you can't live."

"Must I die," she replied, "and not see my mother?" Then she turned to her husband, and asked him a startling question for a bride of less than a week. She said, "Henry, have I ever deceived you?" This simple phrase impressed the balladeers so much that you find it, in some form or other, in every version of the story.

Shortly after this Henry went out on a double errand. First his horse was to be bedded down for the night in the stables adjoining Dennison and Streeter's store, and then there was more arsenic to be filched from the glass jar in the store itself. He carelessly forgot to replace the jar. He says in his confession that the first pangs of remorse came about this time Sunday afternoon when he saw how Mary Ann suffered.

Back in the Hull household Mary Ann told her brother David, who was with her much of the time, that Henry was putting powders in her drinks and that the powders made her sick. Then she asked if she could talk to Doctor Hull. The kindly physician was called to her bedside where he sat close to her, for by this time her voice was so weak that it could hardly be heard. At the trial the doctor testified as follows:

> Mrs. Green said after I sat down by her bed, that after taking those pills which Henry gave her on Friday, she had been in the most awful distress, and it seemed sometimes that she could not live. . . . She says, 'Henry has been feeding me with white powders ever since I took those pills . . . he has put it into my coffee and into my broth, and almost all my drinks, yesterday I asked him for some drink . . . He got some, turned his back to me, took a paper from his pocket and dusted something into it that was white; he gave it to me; I asked him what it was he put into it, and he says a little flour; I drank it and it distressed me very much.'

The doctor then went on to tell how he asked her to repeat to one of the elders of the town, Barzaleel Streeter, what she had just told him. This she did but in so weak a voice that Hull could not easily hear her. At the trial Streeter's testimony substantiated Hull's.

She grew weaker all through Sunday night. At ten o'clock Monday morning, the eighth day after her marriage, Mary Ann Wyatt Green died.

A coroner's jury met in the church. The various witnesses told of the mysterious white powders — white scum on the soup, white sediment in the wine glass, white powder in everything Henry had given his wife. The powder Mrs. Hull had salvaged from the sick room was submitted to a crude but successful test by the watchmaker and the physicians. It was arsenic. Then came surgeons from Troy who removed the stomach, the esophagus, and part of the intestines. These they carried off to the Rensselaer Polytechnic Institute in Troy, where a professor of the chemistry department analyzed the contents. He found arsenic and a great deal of it.

The trial for murder opened in the county seat, Troy, on July 7 at "3½ o'clock p.m." There were four judges, but the court was presided over by Judge Amasa J. Parker. The district attorney and John Van Buren, attorney general of the State of New York, prosecuted. For twelve days the trial went on, attracting increasing public attention. The Troy papers reported the proceedings in full. More than half their news was concerned with the trial. On July 16, the Troy *Daily Whig* had this notice: "To our Readers: The testimony in the criminal case before the Special Oyer and Terminer is so voluminous as to exclude from our columns many interesting items of news. We are also compelled from the same cause to curtail our commercial articles. When the trial shell [*sic*] have been concluded we will make up our leeway."

Papers reported that "the courtroom [was] densely crowded about half the assemblage consisting of ladies . . . some had come from a distance of many miles" (Troy *Daily Whig*, July 19).

The defense was presented by outstanding lawyers, paid, it was repeatedly noted by the state, by Green's wealthy connections. Though it seems unbelievable to one reading the testimony, Green thought his influence and some few flaws in the prosecution would save him.

Day after day the facts piled up against him. The character of his wife, the conversations about arsenic, the jar of arsenic he failed to replace on the shelf, the keen-eyed observations of the village wives who had nursed his wife, Mary Ann's statements to David, the doctor, and Streeter — bit by bit these built a wall of indisputable evidence around Green.

When all was over, Judge Parker summed up the case, carefully and fairly; the jury retired. The verdict was "guilty," and Henry Green was sentenced to hang by the neck until dead on September 10. He gave him the full extent of the law for appeal.

During the weeks that followed, Green's "rich and powerful friends . . . of high respectability and character" brought great pressure to bear upon Governor Silas Wright for executive clemency. The boy was called insane; time was requested for the legislature to change the murder laws; time for Green to prepare adequately for death. But on September 3, Governor Wright wrote the sheriff of Renssalaer County that he was refusing executive clemency despite these requests, despite vague references to violence done one of Green's supporters, and despite equally vague references to the insanity in Green's family.

In the meantime Green was in Troy jail. Sometime in August he helped Hakes, his cellmate, escape from jail. It was Henry who got the key and held the blankets for the other man to slide down. He did not escape himself because he was assured by his lawyers that he would be reprieved.

Beginning August 29, at the request of Green's mother, the Reverend Robert B. Van Kleeck, rector of St. Paul's Episcopal Church, Troy, was in daily attendance upon Henry. Bit by bit the confession was made. When it was published five days after the execution, it cleared up some minor mysteries of the trial and exonerated his mother and Alzina Godfrey of all blame.

The execution on September 10 was all a journalist could hope for, and the writer for the Troy *Whig* had a story that would be the envy of any tabloid editor. He tells how the crowds from distant points flocked into Troy for twenty-four hours preceding the event. It was a "private hanging," but from noon to four o'clock Ferry Street was jammed with two or three thousand spectators, many of them females. The Troy Citizens Corps was called out to guard the jail.

Green himself was weak as he walked to the scaffold with the Reverend R. B. Van Kleeck, Episcopalian, and the Reverend George Baldwin, Baptist. He mounted the scaffold at three-forty o'clock and joined the group of fifty in singing *Rock of Ages Cleft for Me*. The clergymen prayed for his soul and wept while they pressed his hand and left him. The rope was adjusted carefully about his neck. He prayed, throwing himself on God's mercy; the amen being said, Sheriff Gideon Reynolds pulled the pin, the body jumped three or four feet, a slight spasm crossed his face, there were a few convulsions, and the husband and murderer of Mary Ann Wyatt was dead. The Troy *Whig* had no end of praise for Sheriff Reynolds, who was running for re-election on the Whig ticket that fall.

So that is the end of the story except for a strange bit of lore about Mary Ann and her burial. There is a well-substantiated tale of the exhuming of Mary Ann's body about 1885 to make room for building lots. When her coffin came to the surface, it broke open. There lay a whitened skeleton in the midst of rotted cloth, but over the head and shoulders fell cascades of beautiful auburn hair. Only for a moment was it visible, and then a gust of wind shattered it to nothingness, save in the memories of the men who saw it. Another legend says that her teeth were so beautiful that the grave diggers divided them among themselves for souvenirs.

A monument was erected about the time her body was moved; the inscription reads:

This monument is erected by the Citizens of Berlin in memory of Mary Ann Wyatt, wife of Henry G. Green, who was married Feb. 9, 1845 and on the 14th day of the same month was poisoned by her husband with arsenic without any real or pretended cause.

Beautiful, intelligent, and virtuous, she was wept over by the community, and the violated law justly exacted the life of her murderer as a penalty for his crime.

There are seven known versions of this story in ballad form. The best known of these, *Henry Green*, was published by Mrs. Helen Hartness Flanders and Mr. George Brown in their

Vermont Folk-Songs and Ballads (Brattleboro, 1932). That version was recorded from the singing of Mr. Fred Ballard of Jamaica, Vt. This, however, was not the earliest printed verse on this subject.

On the back leaf of the testimony of the trial, printed in July 1845, there is a very sentimental poem, signed M. A. S. I quote two stanzas:

> A poison'd chalice he obtain'd
>   Which to her lips he gave;
> She drank it off, its fatal dregs
>   Were deadly as the grave.
>
> But ere her gentle spirit fled
>   She called him to her side—
> "Oh, Henry, have I e'er deceived?"
>   "No," coldly he replied.

There are certain similarities between this poem and the version transmitted by oral tradition, but this is not the place for a discussion of these.

Mrs. Helen Hartness Flanders, that kindly and generous pioneer collector of Vermont folklore, showed me four versions of the murder, recorded from the singers of her state. With her permission I am printing one of these, called *Mary Wyatt*. This was taken down from the singing of Mr. Elmer George of North Montpelier, Vt. Excepting only the *Henry Green* Mrs. Flanders published, this is the finest of the oral tradition versions.

MARY WYATT

> Come, listen to my tragedy
> Good people young and old,
> An awful story you shall hear
> 'Twill make your blood run cold;
> Concerning a fair damsal—
> Mary Wyatt was her name—
> She was poisoned by her husband
> And he hung for the same.

Mary Wyatt, she was beautiful,
Not of a high degree.
And Henry Green was wealthy
As you may plainly see.
He said, "My dearest Mary,
If you'll become my wife
I will guard you and protect you
Through all this gloom of life."

"O Henry, I would marry you;
I would give my consent,
But before that we'd been married long
I fear you would repent;
Before that we'd been married long,
You'd make me a disgrace
Because I'm not as rich as you
Which ofttimes is the case."

"O Mary, dearest Mary,
How can you grieve me so?
I'll vow and 'clare by all that's fair
I always will prove true;
But unless you consent to become my wife
You'll surely end my life
For no longer do I wish to live
Unless you are my wife."

Believing what he said was true,
She then became his wife.
But little did she think, poor girl,
That he would end her life.
O, little did she think, poor child,
And little did she explain
That he would end her precious life

. . . .

They had not been married but a week or two
When she was taken ill
Great doctors were sent for
To try their powerful skill;
Great doctors were sent for
But none of them could save

And soon it was proclaimed
She must go to her grave.

O, when her brothers heard of this,
Straightway to her did go
Saying, "Sister dear, you're dying,
The doctors tell us so."
Saying, "Sister dear, you're dying;
Your life is at an end."
Saying, "Haven't you been poisoned
By the one you call your friend?"

"I'm on my deathbed lying.
I know that I must die.
I know I'm going before my God
And the truth I won't deny.
I know (my) Henry's poisoned me.
Dear brothers, for him send
For I love him now as dearly
As when he was my friend."

When Henry heard those tidings
Straightaway to his wife to see,
Saying, "Mary my dearest Mary,
Was you ever deceived in me?"
Three times she called, "Dear Henry!"
Then and sank into a swoon
He gazed on her indifferently
And in silence left the room.

"Now Henry has deceiv-ed me.
How my poor heart is wrong!
But when I'm dead and buried, O
Don't have poor Henry hung!
I freely have forgiven him,"
And she turned upon her side.
"In Heaven meet me, Henry"
And she sweetly smiled and died.

Crazy Bill Had a Down Look

Co-author: JAMES TAYLOR DUNN

I T was a great event in the upstate New York villages of the Finger Lakes country, during the late 1840s, when George J. Mastin came to town with his "Unparalleled Exhibition of Oil Paintings." First there appeared broadsides on barn doors and in tavern barrooms describing the fourteen huge paintings (8 × 10 feet, most of them) and promising a religious and historical lecture by Mr. Mastin explaining the paintings; there would also be clog dancing by the Erin Twin Brothers, comic songs, and a demonstration of phrenological reading.

A day or so after the broadsides were posted came the show and its impresario. The paintings, done on bed ticking and rolled up in a long, stout wooden box, were transported from town to town in a farm wagon and carefully hung in the sheds of the local tavern, or in the ballroom, if it were big enough. The show was always at night when twenty flickering candles added movement and excitement to the crude but vivid and forceful work of the unknown artists. Sometimes Mastin would take out his violin and fiddle for dancing. Fiddling and phrenology, lecturing on history and religion were his pastimes; by trade a tailor, he was later to be a country storekeeper and farmer. He lived a long life over in Genoa and Sempronius, from 1814 to 1910, and seems to have enjoyed himself all the way.

111

A man could understand without any difficulty the pictures that George Mastin had hired some good sign or carriage painters to do for him. When he lectured before each picture, it all seemed very moving and very real. Five of the canvases were scenes right out of the Bible. Then there were five exciting pictures from American history. But the great drawing card was the series of four which depicted in horrifying, bloody detail the murder of the spectators' own good neighbor, John G. Van Nest, his wife, his baby son, and mother-in-law—all four of them brutally stabbed to death in a few minutes by that crazy colored fellow, Bill Freeman, in their home just south of Auburn.

From mid-March 1846 to the summer of 1847, the Van Nest murders were a favorite topic of conversation in those parts. They raised a lot of questions. For example, how could you tell if a man was crazy? And if he was crazy and committed a murder, was that any reason not to hang him? And why would a man like former Governor William H. Seward, one of the leading lawyers in the state, of his own accord and for no fee, defend this villian?

Bill Freeman was born in the small upstate New York village of Auburn in September 1823, and all the cards were stacked against him from the beginning. His father, who died insane, was a freed slave; his mother, part Negro, part Indian, was a heavy drinker. One uncle became a wandering lunatic, and an aunt died early and mad. Despite the fact that Auburn was to become a station of the Underground Railroad and the home of its most famous conductor, Harriet Tubman, it was also a community which long retained strong Copperhead sympathies. The colored population was completely isolated, without any benefits from cultural influences and deprived of the privileges of church and school.

When he reached the age of seven, young Bill was put out to work as a servant boy. He was remembered from this time as being not much different from any other boy—lively, smart, and active. At times he was lazy, trying to avoid work, and occasionally he ran away. He laughed, played, was good natured, and "talked like other folks."

During those difficult, formative years, Freeman came

under no good influences. Three times he was arrested for minor offenses, first when he broke open a peddler's cart in front of the Bank Coffee House. A short while later he fled via canal boat after stealing some of Jonas Underwood's chickens, was quickly apprehended and brought back.

In the spring of 1840, the Widow Godfrey of Sennett Township, five miles north of Auburn, lost a horse. Young Bill Freeman, then in his middle teens, was suspected and arrested but freed after examination by a local magistrate. Some weeks later the Godfrey horse turned up in Chemung County where it had been sold by another Auburn Negro, Jack Furman. Furman, who knew of Freeman's previous arrest, immediately accused the youth. On Furman's testimony Bill Freeman was convicted and sentenced to five years in prison.

From September 1840 to the same month five years later, Freeman was locked up at the State Prison in Auburn. During the first year of his imprisonment, Keeper James E. Tyler ordered Freeman flogged for not doing his full quota of work. Instead of complying with Tyler's order to strip, Freeman attacked the keeper who took a piece of basswood board a half-inch thick and struck the prisoner over the head, splitting the plank. This was followed by a heavy flogging.

From this point on Freeman's mood darkened and a serious deafness developed (a postmortem was to disclose a diseased temporal bone and a broken eardrum). "It was as though the stones of my ears dropp'd down," he stated, "as if the sound went down my throat." Orders had to be given several times before he would understand, and seldom did he hold up his head and look a man in the face. "Crazy Bill," the keepers commented, "always had a down look."

His sense of betrayal, bitterness, and loneliness added to the misunderstanding of others. The foreman of the dye house considered Freeman " a being of very low, degraded intellect, hardly above a brute, and I treated him so." Whenever Freeman would cry that the floggings hurt him so he couldn't sleep, they would lay the cat on his back with added force.

When Freeman was released from the Auburn State Prison on September 20, 1845, few people recognized him. For the next five and a half months he earned what living he could by sawing wood, although few wanted to employ him. For his room he helped his landlady, Mary Ann Newark, carry laundry up from the New Guinea section of Auburn to the village. At home he always sat and but seldom spoke. If he said anything, it was mostly about their not paying him at prison. He felt that since he had been put away without cause, he should have his full recompense for those five years of hard work. "There wouldn't anybody pay me," he kept brooding.

It wasn't until March of the following year that Freeman decided to do something about this injustice. First, he visited the farm of Martha Godfrey whose stolen horse had sent him to prison. He ate a cake she put out for him but could bring himself to say nothing of his grievances. Later he stopped for five minutes at a home three miles south of Auburn, a well-kept frame farmhouse on the road which skirts the west shore of Owasco Lake. Here at John Van Nest's he asked unsuccessfully for a job. Freeman next sought a warrant for the arrest of the man (or men—he couldn't make himself clear) who had put him in jail. At the Auburn office of Magistrate Lyman Paine he flew into a passion when this demand was refused.

The dark storm brewing in his twisted mind became more oppressive. On Monday, March 9, Freeman purchased a knife. On March 12, he said to himself, "I must begin my work," the work of vengeance and requital. Reaching Owasco Lake, he took the shore road down to the west side. He paused at two or three places, but it wasn't far enough out to begin. The moon came up, shimmering on the recently fallen snow. It was cold. When Freeman reached the farmhouse of John G. Van Nest, he decided that the time had come. Here was where he should begin his work.

Within the house the Van Nest family was preparing for bed. It was almost 9:30, and a visiting neighbor had just left. The master of the house, forty-one-year-old John G. Van Nest, justice of the peace, supervisor, and highly respected farmer, was warming himself in front of the stove in the back kitchen. His wife Sarah was about to step out the back door. His mother-in-law, Mrs. Phebe Wyckoff, had taken their oldest child Peter and retired to the north front bedroom. Helen Holmes, Mrs. Wyckoff's great-niece and adopted daughter, had gone with

The unknown artist used as his source a woodcut in the *Cayuga Tocsin*, April 6, 1846, which showed only the house, while he has added old Mrs. Wyckoff slashing Freeman's wrist after being wounded. Mrs. Van Nest, already stabbed, goes toward the house. All four paintings 8′ x 10′ on bed ticking, c. 1847, reproduced through the courtesy of the New York State Historical Association, Cooperstown.

young Julia Van Nest to their bedroom. Cornelius Van Arsdale, the new hired man, was already upstairs, and the youngest in the family, two-year-old George Washington Van Nest, was asleep in the sitting room.

Freeman walked around to the rear of the house. As he approached the door of the back kitchen Mrs. Van Nest stepped out. He met her with a strong upward sweep of his knife, inflicting a single deep wound in her abdomen. Screaming, she ran to the front of the house, was let in, collapsed on a bed, and died a few minutes later. Freeman immediately entered the back door, where he met Mr. Van Nest who died almost instantly, stabbed in the chest and the heart. The murderer then struck the sleeping two-year-old baby George with such ferocity that the knife passed completely through the body. He next attacked the hired man.

Though severely wounded in the breast, Van Arsdale managed to drive Freeman from the house. Out in the yard the murderer slashed seventy-year-old Mrs. Wyckoff, who had armed herself with a butcher knife and run outdoors. Badly wounded, she nevertheless managed to cut Freeman's wrist so severely that, as he later said, "My hand was so hurt, I couldn't kill anymore." Clad only in a flannel nightgown, the undaunted old lady fled across field a quarter mile to the next neighbor south to spread the alarm. In the meantime, within the house Van Arsdale stumbled to the parlor floor where he slumped against the wall while Julia Van Nest and Helen Holmes tried to comfort the dying Georgie. All reason gone, Freeman came back to the house, kicked at the door, peered in the window, and then was gone into the night. Two days later Mrs. Wyckoff died at Brooks' farmhouse, bringing Freeman's toll to four.

Within a matter of minutes after the massacre began, Freeman was on his way, riding Mrs. Wyckoff's aged and uncertain horse down the road toward Auburn. The animal did not last long. Just the other side of the village it fell, and Freeman stabbed the beast for hurting him. He stole another horse and continued the flight to Schroeppel, in the southern part of Oswego County, which he reached at two in the afternoon.

At Schroeppel he was arrested. On Saturday morning the prisoner was driven to the Van Nest home, where he was greeted by an excited, revengeful mob demanding that he be lynched.

By moving fast, however, the authorities were able to spirit Freeman away in a covered wagon. A terrible commotion followed him into the village of Auburn and as the wife of former Governor William H. Seward wrote in a letter to her sister, "I trust in the mercy of God that I shall never again be a witness to such an outburst of the spirit of vengeance as I saw while they were carrying the murderer past our door."

The first voice of reason to be raised was that of a clergy-

The depiction of the murder of little George, with his dead father on the floor. C. 1847, reproduced through the courtesy of the New York State Historical Association, Cooperstown.

man, Reverend John M. Austin of Auburn's Universalist Church; while deploring the murders, his pity went out to the demented Negro and placed the blame on the indifference of the community to their colored population: "Is not society in some degree accountable for this sad catastrophe?"

He characterized the Auburn Negroes as "victims of unworthy prejudices which compel them to exist under circumstances where they are exposed to imbibe all the vices, without being able to become inbued with the virtues of those around them; who can wonder that they fall into crime?" John DePuy, Freeman's brother-in-law, testified that white men had made this murderer what he was, "a brute beast; they don't make anything else of any of our People but brute beasts; but when

Helen Holmes and Julia Van Nest concern themselves with the dead
George, while the wounded Van Arsdale leans against the wall. Looking through the window from the porch is Freeman. C. 1847, reproduced through the courtesy of the New York State Historical Association, Cooperstown.

we violate their laws, then they want to punish us as if we were
men."

Another voice in the wilderness was that of former Governor Seward, then a private lawyer and Auburn's most influential citizen. When no one would undertake the defense of Freeman he offered his services, thereby bringing the wrath of the
entire village down upon him. Seward held the viewpoint, not
yet generally accepted, that the insane were not responsible for
their acts.

Judge Bowen Whiting announced on June 24 that there
would be a preliminary jury trial to determine Freeman's san-

ity. Seward and his law partners volunteered their gratuitous services and appeared for the prisoner. State Attorney General John Van Buren, son of Martin Van Buren, and the district attorney of Cayuga County represented the people. The trial lasted ten days, and in spite of the tremendous evidence of Freeman's insanity, the jurors brought in the verdict that the prisoner was "sufficiently sane in mind and memory, to distinguish between right and wrong."

On July 10, Freeman went before a second jury, this time on trial for his life. Once again the best of authorities were presented by Seward in an attempt to persuade the jury that the murderer was completely insane.

The trial itself was a travesty, where every possible insult and calumny was heaped on Freeman and on his defense. Even Seward's masterful summation, which was called the most impassioned that ever passed his lips, went almost unheard. On the twenty-third Freeman was quickly found guilty, and the following morning Judge Whiting sentenced him to be hanged on September 18.

Seward, continuing his valiant fight on behalf of Freeman, obtained a stay of execution. In October Mrs. Seward paid a visit to the jail with her husband. There she found Freeman with only a few feeble glimmerings of memory. "I was affected to tears by his helpless condition," she wrote to her sister. "I pray God that he may be insensible to the inhumanity of his relentless keepers. He stood upon the cold stone floor with bare feet, a cot bedstead with nothing but the sacking underneath and a small filthy blanket to cover him."

It was on February 11, 1847, that the State Supreme Court handed down a ruling reversing the judgment of the local court and ordering a new trial. In a letter written four days later, Seward called on Dr. Amariah Brigham, head of the State Lunatic Asylum in Utica to submit the names of "one hundred of the most intelligent physicians throughout the State of New York and abroad" who might give evidence. But no trial was ordered. Area newspapers continued to enmesh the case in local politics. They even accused all concerned of taking part in a Whig conspiracy to build up Seward.

To ailing, demented Freeman, languishing in his cell at

As suggested in the text, several of the spectators may be specific portraits; others may be the stereotypes described in contemporary books of physiognomy. C. 1847, reproduced through the courtesy of the New York State Historical Association, Cooperstown.

the Cayuga County jail, his feet heavily ironed, all this meant nothing. For many weeks he had been failing, and those who saw him were convinced that he had become a perfect idiot. He died on Saturday morning, August 21, 1847. A postmortem examination was held, and Dr. Brigham summed up the sad case of Bill Freeman in these few words: "I have very rarely found so extensive disease of the brain in those who have died after long continued insanity, as we found in this instance; and I believe there are few cases of chronic insanity recorded in books, in which were noticed more evident marks of disease."

The great furor created by crazy Bill Freeman was in its

time spread far and wide by the press, but certainly no reporting could have compared with the sense of immediacy and intimacy that came to those who saw the events dramatized in George Mastin's paintings. The last of the series of paintings helps to date them, for the hanging never took place, though it was fully expected until Freeman's death in August 1847. So the date must be after the trial and before his death. The garment Freeman is wearing is the regulation outfit for those about to be hanged. Comparisons with contemporary photographs identify the second and third persons from the left as Governor and Mrs. Seward. I would suggest that the black man on the right triptych may be Jack Furman. The nicest touch of all is the pickpocket, right front.

Rulloff, The Learned Ruffian

THE American Philological Association is one of the oldest scholarly societies in the United States, having been founded during a three-day convention in July 1869. The meeting drew to Poughkeepsie, New York, many of the most distinguished language professors in America and Europe. The principal subjects for discussion were the best methods of teaching foreign languages and that perennial theme for debate, the pronunciation of classical tongues.

It all went very smoothly. The speeches, if a little long, were frequently seasoned with pleasant jokes — puns, often in Latin and Greek. The younger men met the great names, and the men behind the great names met each other. They all had a chance to look over youthful Vassar College and, except for one or two minor incidents, one would have said the gathering an unmitigated success. There was that odd business of the "mysterious disappearances" — Professor Comfort lost his hat and cane, someone else seems to have misplaced his umbrella, and papers were missing from the secretary's desk, all this one could explain; everyone knows how absent minded professors are — but when a reporter from the local paper discovered that some of his notes were missing, it made a body think twice. Nobody at a gathering of philologists would steal anything, but it certainly was odd.

Then there was the unpleasant business of Mr. Euri Leurio. The trouble was, Mr. Leurio just did not belong at that meeting; some of the more worldly may have suspected that their friends the ethnologists had put him up to coming, for word had gone 'round about a meeting of ethnologists in New York he had attended and spoken to and bored the poor fellows half to death with his great "plan." At Poughkeepsie he was everywhere, urging, cajoling, hinting to the scholars that he had a world-shaking formula for the philologists of the world.

Finally he was given the floor on Thursday morning after the entire convention had finished touring Vassar College. The professors had been putting him off as long as possible, but there was a bright gleam in his hazel eyes, a bullying persistence that was hard to deny. He limped slightly as he came forward to stand before them in his plain, well-brushed clothes, a rock of a man, short and bull necked, his great head and gray beard thrust forward as he spoke, the gestures of his hands quick and precise. They had been given an inkling of what was coming from the handbills he had been distributing among them, reprinted from recent editions of the New York dailies. The literary style was hardly calculated to speak to them in their own language:

> Great Discovery — Method in the Formation of Language — Ancient Greek Restored — The Mystery of the Modern Languages Explained — Five Thousand Examples taken Indiscriminately from the Greek, Latin, German, French and English Languages. Their formation rendered as perfectly plain and familiar as if we had made them ourselves — Manuscript for Sale. price $500,000.

It was the last line, of course, that shocked and amused and made clear to one and all that Mr. Euri Leurio, born, as he said, in Canada and — he was a mite vague about this — formerly professor in a western college — did not belong in the world of academe.

Language, he explained, had not developed slowly according to man's need, it had been devised at a meeting of priests and wise men in some distant moment before history began. Out of the conclave had come an elegant, philosophic, artistic method which had been lost but now was rescued by the speaker and, skipping from language to language — he seemed familiar with a good many — he hinted at the whole scheme. For a piddling half million dollars he would sell this work of his lifetime to the newborn American Philological Association.

One can imagine the uncomfortable shifting in their seats as the professors smiled behind their great beards, the sly winks at their friends. But they hadn't elected Professor William D. Whitney, president of Yale College, their president for nothing; he knew exactly what to do. He appointed a committee; what college president could have done less? And not a committee of nonentities either: President J. H. Raymond of Vassar, Professor A. Harkness of Brown University, and the Honorable Porter G. Bliss but recently returned from his difficulties as consul in Paraguay. Young Mr. Bliss was chairman, and however much his name had been recently in the press, Mr. (or if you prefer, Professor) Leurio had apparently never heard of him. After the meeting the two sat together for an hour or so while the young scholar-diplomat tried to make some sense out of the great kitchen-midden of Leurio's mind and out of the huge manuscript he had brought with him and guarded so carefully. At length Leurio came to realize that Bliss knew "absolutely nothing of philology," that he was, to use Leurio's own favorite word, a humbug. The committee decided that Mr. Leurio's proposal did not come within the objectives of the convention, and it was turned down; with great tact the report was not included in the minutes of the convention. So the discordant note was silenced, and Mr. Leurio packed up his papers and went back to New York.

How could the good professors have known what a blow they had rendered? Leurio had expected that Poughkeepsie would be the scene of a great triumph, the crown placed on his years of work, his study in cold, lonely rooms, his hours at the Eclectic, the Mercantile, and the Astor libraries in New York, his long nights pouring over lexicons and classical texts. He was angry at the blindness, the stupidity of these pedantic, self-assuming fellows, and he would stay angry to his dying day.

There were others to share his dismay, loyal friends who might not understand entirely what the professor was up to but whose hearts were with him, in some instances, their hearts and hands. To his landlady, Mrs. Jacobs at 170 Third Avenue, he was like the scholarly rabbis of her youth in the old country — always poring over his books, studying, writing. She held him up to her son Edward as a model, and she encouraged her fourteen-year-old daughter to sit at his feet and learn something about the languages he knew so well. He was always quiet, always charming, never drunk, no noisy card games, no trouble; the absolutely perfect boarder.

About those other friends — one was a young man of about thirty, of unusual attractiveness, bright, studious, competent in Latin and French who lived in the small apartment with the professor and was known to the Jacobs as Charles G. Curtis. There was another friend called Dexter who visited them on occasion, of quite a different stripe — rough, uncouth, really quite unpleasant but obviously devoted to Leurio. What the Jacobs did not know — among many other things — was that the money for his rent came exclusively from the endeavors of these two younger men to whom Leurio was advisor, guide, philosopher, and mentor. But, then, there was so much the Jacobs didn't know!

Euri Leurio was born in 1819 at Hammond River, New Brunswick, to William Rulloffson and his wife, Pricilla Howard, and he was baptised Edward Howard Rulloffson, a name he later shortened to Rulloff (or Ruloff, sometimes). His father died when the boy was five or so, leaving three sons and a daughter. Pricilla Rulloffson was a devout woman who brought Edward up in the Episcopal Church and soon discovered that he was a great reader with an unquenchable thirst for knowledge in mathematics, *belle lettres*, and especially for ancient and modern languages. He skipped through the Academy in St. John, New Brunswick, graduating way ahead of those his age, a lonely book-worm, with no playmates, no young confidantes, no sense of play. A boy who read through the night, if allowed. There was no more money for schooling; his mother had remarried, and a fifth child was to be cared for.

He went to work in the store of Keator and Thorne in St. John; shortly afterward there were two fires in that store, and later writers would suggest that Edward Rulloff was responsible, without any proof that I have seen. For three years he worked as clerk in a law office of a distinguished barrister, Duncan Robertson, learning a great deal about common law which he would put to good use in the years ahead. Then *something* discreditable happened — there were later a variety of explanations but none very explicit from him, and in 1841 he left St. John, wandered awhile in the provinces, thence to New York. Some writers have suggested that this was after two years in a New Brunswick prison, but that may or may not be true.

In New York he attended a business school run by a man named Gourand, whom Rulloff later also damned as a humbug; apparently Gourand had promised a job upon graduation and failed to deliver. This is probably where Rulloff learned shorthand and bookkeeping. In the spring of 1842, he took a steamboat to Albany and worked his way to Syracuse on a canal boat. It was there that he met a boatman named Schutt, from whom he got a job on one of the boats going south to Cayuga Lake; thence he went to Dryden where Schutt's family was kind to him and probably somewhat awed by him, this young Canadian who knew foreign languages, the law, business methods, and so much else. He could be absolutely charming, and it was some time before they glimpsed his capacity for anger that could transform him.

He said he wanted to teach but, while biding his time for an opening, he clerked in an Ithaca druggist shop, harnessing his zeal for learning to drugs and all the mysteries of that trade. Then he taught in a select school in Dryden for a term, and one of his pupils was young Harriet Schutt who fell in love with him — and insofar as that was possible, he with her. Then he studied botanical medicine with a Dr. Stone. He also took up the new "science" of phrenology and gave a public lecture on the subject, reading from his shorthand notes. There seemed to be no end to his accomplishments.

And yet there was uneasiness — especially on the part of Harriet's mother who saw and sensed more than the rest of the family. There was Rulloff's intense jealousy of Dr. W. H. Bull, a young man with orthodox medical views who was distantly related to the Schutts and acted far more familiarly with the girls of the house than Rulloff considered proper. He even kissed them — and once even kissed Harriet. This was a bone of contention but, nevertheless, Harriet and Edward Rulloff were married December 31, 1843. Discord and recriminations increased, but shortly the couple moved to Lansing a few miles away. Edward was practicing botanic medicine and doing some teaching; his library had increased. The little house was well furnished, and neighbors saw only the appearance of peaceful harmony. In April of '45, a baby, Pricilla, was born to them, named after Edward's mother. Two months later Harriet's brother called Edward to come and examine his wife and child, both of whom were very sick, and in a few days both died. Years later the bodies were dug up, and the stomachs chemically tested for poison, but nothing at that date, could be proved to implicate Edward in their deaths.

Actually life was not so peaceful as it seemed. Harriet by this time had learned the calibre of the anger of which her husband was capable. Pulled one way by her family, the other by her marriage, this girl of nineteen was caught in a classic trap. Let Edward tell what happened the night of June 23, 1845, as he remembered it twenty-eight years later:

> I told her that I had got hold of a little money: that I was going west to find something profitable to do, and that I wished that she would remain there and keep house until my return, or until I sent for her; that I had been in correspondence with persons in Ohio, and I expected to get to be a Principal of an Academy out there; that I intended to drop practising medicine, and to become, in time, either a Professor in a College, or a lawyer. Harriet said that she would never go to Ohio, or so far away from her family, that if I went away she would not remain and keep house, and that she would take her child and things and go home, that she was tired of living with me any how, and that her mother was anxious for her to return home. Of course this made me very angry, it rather upset my plans, and I did not know what to do. I could not make a decent living there; my practice amounted to nothing, and I had no taste for it; besides, I was poor, and too proud to have the neighbors and people generally know how poor I was. Angry words ensued between us. I accused Harriet of wanting to see Dr. Bull, and told her that she thought more of him

than she did of me. She said she had a right to if she so desired, that he was *her cousin*. At this I told her that she might go where she pleased. I think I said she might go to h — —l if she chose to, but that she should not take the child, that I would take care of that. At this I attempted to take the child away from her, and she clung to it. In my passion I reached for the pestal of the mortar in which I pounded medicines, and which stood near by, and struck her with it over the left temple. I must have struck very hard — I was a young man and very strong, and the blow broke her skull. She fell senseless with the child still in her arms, which was crying. Oh! that dreadful hour! that horrible moment which I would have given worlds to blot out! It makes me — *yes, even me* — shudder sometimes when I think of it.

Rulloff was a classic liar, but this time I believe him. Once, years later, a chest of his was opened in Chicago and among books and papers was one containing a lock of light brown hair and written on the paper, "a lock of Harriet's hair. Oh! that dreadful hour!" But it will be noticed that he says nothing of the child, and he never admitted killing her, although it seems entirely likely that during his rage the child either accidently or intentionally was killed. In any event, she was never seen again, and in none of the trials which followed did the truth come out.

In his *Confession* Rulloff claimed that that night he considered suicide — but not for long. He emptied a chest he owned, wrapped Harriet in two sheets and bed ticking, added some flatirons and the fatal mortar, crowded the lot into the chest, and closed the lid. (Was the child's corpse there too?) Next morning he borrowed a horse and wagon from his neighbors, the Robertsons, who helped him load the chest on the wagon, remarking on its weight. He had a cock and bull story to explain his wife's absence and the presence of the chest, then he drove off slowly toward Cayuga Lake, going on back roads until he reached the shore, then south around Ithaca and north along the west shore, where he stole a boat, took the chest to it, adding stones and pieces of iron, rowed to a spot he believed to be the deepest spot in the lake, and dropped the contents of the chest overboard which was never after to be seen by anyone.

The disposal of the body (or bodies) was in the night of June 24, and the next morning he slowly drove back to Lansing and was seen to lift the box off the wagon bed without any difficulty and put it in the house. He returned the horse to the Robertsons, saying that he and his wife would be visiting "between the lakes" for two or three weeks—an expression in those parts to mean between two of the Finger Lakes. Laughingly he told his neighbor, "Please don't let anyone carry away our house while we are gone."

Rulloff shared with many criminals a compulsion to place himself in danger of discovery after his crimes. This time he walked in the June sun to Ithaca and visited William Schutt and Jane Schutt who was housekeeping for her brother since his wife's death. Rulloff offered his brother-in-law a ring the latter had once given Harriet—William said to return it to Harriet. He rented a horse and wagon in Ithaca, returned to Lansing, filled two boxes this time, one with things to sell, including clothing of his wife's, the other with books and papers. That night he returned the horse and took the stage to Geneva, then on to Rochester, Buffalo, and finally to Chicago. He sold the contents of the first box, and in Chicago he pawned the second for $30; it was in this one that finally the lock of Harriet's hair was found. He could find no work and no rest for, as he said in his *Confession*, "I was constantly haunted by some terrible visage awake or asleep. Remorse, remorse pursued one everywhere."

Summer week followed summer week and no word of the Rulloffs came east. Various people—some of them Schutts—went out to the house in Lansing only to find it closed and the blinds shut. Eventually the door was forced, and the interior found to be in utter confusion. In Ithaca and Dryden more and more people began to feel that their local intellectual had in some way done away with his wife and child. On August 4, a group of men—including two of the Schutts—were discussing this whole puzzling problem in Hale's store in Ithaca, when the door opened, and there stood Dr. Edward H. Rulloff himself. They plied him with questions, at first relieved by his presence and by his assurance that his wife was "between the lakes."

If Rulloff was a compulsive liar, he was also consistently an imprudent one. At dinner with William Schutt that night he said Harriet was near Erie, Pennsylvania; later when he went to Dryden to stay with his father- and mother-in-law he changed his story again, now Harriet was in Madison, Ohio, where she liked the climate and society and where he had been engaged to teach. He may have been able to con the men in the Schutt family but not their mother, Hannah Schutt. She believed he was lying and drove him out of her house in no gentle fashion. He went back to William's place in Ithaca, where he was already afraid of either a mob or the police, and he then lit out for the west again, with Ephraim Schutt, another of Harriet's brothers, close on his heels. Schutt finally caught up with him in the last car of a train standing in the Rochester station. Rulloff said he would take him to Harriet. In Buffalo, as they were in the crowd getting on the boat, Rulloff vanished and was nowhere to be found on the boat.

Ephraim went on to Erie where a brother lived, thence to Madison, Ohio — no word of Harriet. But he picked up a warrant for Rulloff's arrest and found him in a saloon in Cleveland, where he had him arrested by a celebrated and highly experienced detective, known as "Old Hayes" whom Rulloff set about to charm into releasing him. Young Schutt outwitted him and had him locked in a strong room on the boat that carried them back to Buffalo. By this time Rulloff had assumed an air of injured innocence; his wife and child were alive and well, but he would not be treated this way, and he wouldn't give them any more information than that. Finally, Ephraim brought him back to Ithaca in handcuffs, and he was locked in the Tompkins County jail. Since no *corpus delecti* had been located, he was indicted on a charge of abducting his wife and tried in January 1846.

The trial was a major event, and the court was crowded every day. Rulloff's only defense was based on legal technicalities, and the jury's quick verdict was "guilty," with the judge committing him to ten years of hard labor in Auburn State Prison. During that decade, from 1846 to 1856, he spent as much time as possible reading what was available in the prison library, especially everything related to languages. He studied the Greek testament, not for religious but for philological reasons. The prison authorities found him amazingly versatile in all the mechanical shops, with a knack for improving techniques. He worked in the shop where they made ingrained carpets and soon replaced the outside French artist who did their designing, thus saving the state some $5,000 a year. From his own viewpoint the most important event was that he got his first insight to his theory of the formation of language which was to be his lodestar for the rest of his life. Ten years were a long time, and like any prisoner he looked forward to their ending, but when, on January 25, 1856, he went to the warden's office to be released, there stood the new sheriff of Tompkins County with a warrant for his arrest for the murder of his wife.

The sentence he had just served was for her abduction, now they would try to hang him for her muder, but after considerable legal maneuvering they changed the indictment and charged him with the murder of his daughter. The prosecution had no *corpus delicti*, which Lord Hale long ago had said was essential to conviction, but other circumstances surrounding her disappearance seemed convincing enough. So persuaded was practically everyone in Tompkins County that Rulloff was guilty, that they moved the trial to Owego in neighboring Tioga County. The jury found him guilty, and he was sentenced to be hanged. The sentence was appealed to higher courts.

In the meantime Rulloff was back in the jail at Ithaca where the under sheriff, a man named Jacob Jarvis was in charge. He was a good deal of a brute, this Jarvis, bullying his wife and abusing Rulloff of whom he became jealous, whether with reason or not it is hard to tell. Certainly Ithaca thought Rulloff seduced her, which he always denied, but in a different sense he did seduce sixteen-year-old Albert Jarvis. Authorities let Rulloff teach some young people German and Latin in his cell, among them this lad, bright and active but also impulsive and rash; Albert became totally devoted to the older man so that a symbiotic relationship developed that lasted to the night when Jarvis drowned in the Chenango River, thirteen years later. Inevitably one asks if there was a homosexual relationship between the two; from the evidence available I doubt it. As a matter of fact, Rulloff's sexual drives never appear to have been very strong.

One of the reasons why it was thought that Mrs. Jarvis was having an affair with Rulloff was that the night she and Albert disappeared so too did Rulloff after Albert pulled the bolt on Rulloff's cell. They seem, however, to have gone in different directions, the Jarvises into western New York and Rulloff southwest into Pennsylvania. The details of the first months after his escape are foggy, but in due time he appeared in Meadville, Pennsylvania, where he made friends with the president of Alleghany College and through him with the faculty and the local establishment. He seemed to them to be a learned gentleman, blessed with a brilliant intellect, professionally at ease with the local lawyers and physicians. One day he dropped in on a man of considerable and varied learning named A. B. Richmond, Esq., from whom we catch a glimpse of Rulloff's ability to charm and impress. This is the way Richmond remembered the events, (from Edward Crapsee, *A Man of Two Lives* [New York, 1871]):

> It was in the winter time, about twelve years ago, that I was sitting in my office, when a man came in, dressed in cheap, plain garments, looking like a farmer, and asked if this was Mr. Richmond. I replied that it was, when he said that he had heard that I had invented a patent machine, and wished to know if I would be willing to get an agent to sell it for me. He said his name was James Nelson; that, although a stranger to me, yet he could give me undoubted references as to character, &c. There was something peculiar in this man's appearance. He had a face the most peculiar I ever saw; a face once seen, never to be forgotten. I saw from the tone of his voice that he was evidently a gentleman of culture and education. I took him into my laboratory to show him the machine. He seemed pleased with it, and wished me to make him a proposition. As the machine was one that I had invented more as a matter of pastime than for profit, without any intention or thought of pecuniary recompense, I told him that I would give him the undivided half interest of the United States for $500.

He said he would take it, that he had a brother who was quite wealthy, and would assist him, and he would get the money when he got the model ready. I asked him if he could construct a model. "Yes," said he, "I am a fine mechanic;" and with the science of which he seemed thoroughly conversant.

We went into my collection room, and first came to a case containing marine shells. The shells had been lying on cards, and some visitors who had been examining them had transposed them. He immediately stopped and called my attention to the fact, saying, "Mr. Richmond, that is certainly not correct. That shell is not correctly labelled. That shell is surely not Spondylus Spinosus, but is the Argonanti Argo." I discovered the mistake, perceiving how it had occured. Of course I was very much astonished to find that he should know anything about them, but I found, upon further conversation, that he was perfectly familiar with the science of conchology, and also equally well acquainted with the science of mineralogy. My astonishment increased, when, a little further along, he picked up the skull of an Indian that had been found on a Western battlefield, and remarked, "Ah, that man received a terrible blow upon the right *parietal* bone. See, it has fractured the temporal bone;" and remarked further, "He must have been a man of considerable age, as the *lambdiodal suture* is almost obliterated." Upon further conversation with him, I found that he was a fine anatomist, a science to which I had paid some attention. We passed then to the case of insects, and I found that he was likewise acquainted with the science of entomology, naming the insects in my collection as readily as I could.

By this time my surprise was unbounded, as I had had many learned men visit my collection, but never found one that seemed to understand so well all the sciences connected with the objects in my museum. He passed around the collection and repeated a quotation in Latin, with which, by mere chance, I happened to be familiar, and I continued the conversation as though he had spoken to me in English. Then he repeated a sentence in Greek. I discovered that he was evidently trying to exhibit his best phases intellectually, and remarked to him that it was something unusual to find a visitor so well acquainted with the sciences and languages. He then took from his pocket a certificate from the late Rev. Dr. Barker, President of Allegheny College. The certificate stated that he had examined Mr. James Nelson in Latin, Greek, Hebrew, French, and German, and that he took pleasure in stating "that he found him one of the best linguists it was ever his pleasure to meet." Nelson said that he had obtained the certificate, as he desired to obtain the situation of principal in some school or academy. We then passed into the laboratory, where we found on a shelf some apparatus that I had used in the stomach of Daniel Drewer, who had been poisoned by arsenic. I found him perfectly familiar with all the tests for detecting poisons, and apparently as much so with my galvanic, electrical, magnetic, and chemical apparatus as I was myself, or even more so.

I completed the arrangement with him for the sale of the patent, and told him that a townsman of mine, one George Stewart, had also invented a machine, and that I did not doubt but he could get the agency of that machine also. He effected an arrangement with Stewart, and on the next day went to work to construct a model of my machine. That evening when I left my office I left him at work in the laboratory, and in the morning when looking out, I saw a light still there, and when I went in I found him still at work. He gave as his reason for working all night, that his eyes were weak, and he was better able to work at night than in the daylight. He had partially constructed a beautiful model, which was also exquisitely carved and ornamented. He worked at that model for several weeks, working always at night.

In going into the laboratory one day, he asked me if I had any emery wheel, for polishing. I showed him one, which he said was not rightly constructed, and described to me a method of constructing one which I had heard was used in the Auburn Penitentiary, in the State of New York. I remarked to him, jocularly, "Mr. Nelson, that is the way they polish cutlery in the penitentiary. Were you ever in there?" He turned suddenly upon me, and his eyes fairly blazed with fire, with a look like a tiger ready to spring upon its victim, as he said, "What do you mean?" and a more fiendish expression on a human countenance I think I never saw. But he perceived from my look that it was only in joke. He said that he had seen that one in use for polishing cutlery, when there on a visit.

A few days after this he informed me that it would be difficult for him to get money, and wished to know if I would take four or five gold watches as payment in the place of money, stating that he could get them easily. By that time I had become so much attached to the man that I would have let him have the invention upon any terms. I said I would. He stated that he would go and see his brother in a few days, but before doing so wished to attend our Court of Oyer and Terminer, which was to sit the next week, knowing that I was to defend a man for murder during that term of court. He attended the court and manifested an intense degree of interest in that trial for murder.

He asked me, then, if a man could be convicted of murder without positive proof of what lawyers term the *corpus delecti*, or that the murder had been actually committed, by the actual finding of the body? This was a question in which he seemed very much interested.

A few days after he went away, as he said, to see his brother, taking with him some handbills, which he had got printed, advertising my invention and that of Mr. Stewart. He borrowed five dollars of his landlord, and on the night he left, a boot and shoe store near his hotel was broken open and some boots and leather taken therefrom. In a day or two his landlord received five dollars from him by mail, from a little town in the country a few miles distant, and where he ascertained that a man answering to his description had sold some boots and leather. A few days after, our postmaster received a letter from Warren county, Pa., stating that a jewelry store had been broken open, and some watches taken, which were afterwards found concealed in a pile of lumber, with one of those handbills wrapped around them. This led to inquiry of our postmaster as to whether two men resided in Meadville, named, respectively, A. B. Richmond and George Stewart, and inquiring as to their character, etc. Mr. Stewart, when informed by the postmaster of the circumstances, was very much annoyed, as he was a most exemplary member of one of our most prominent churches, and I annoyed him still more by informing him that there was pretty strong evidence against us that we had committed the burglary. Mr. Stewart recollected that Nelson had had his photograph taken in this place, and immediately had one printed and sent down to Warren county, whence we shortly after received information that James Nelson was the celebrated Edward H. Rulloff, who, it was suspected, had murdered his wife and child in Ithaca, N.Y.

One incident took place in the period when he was trying to escape after the jewelry and leather robberies. Hastening through the winter night on foot he was very cold, and a day or two later he discovered that he had frozen two toes so badly that they had to be removed, an accident that years later was to slip a noose around his neck.

Two observations about the robberies. Rulloff was unquestionably a very bright man, but he was an unbelievably careless burglar. Only such — or a fool — would wrap his loot in broadsides that scores of people would identify with him. Or was it his old compulsion to be caught, to leave so marked a trail that his punishment was inevitable? And of course they did catch him, teaching in a writing school in Ohio, where he tried to kill the constable who arrested him with a three-barreled pistol he had invented. They spirited him back to Ithaca, where the sheriff secretly took him to Auburn Prison, having been forewarned of an angry mob that would try to hang him. But while he had been gone, the court of appeals had decided in his favor, reaffirming that without a *corpus delicti* there could be no conviction for murder, and so he was free to go his way.

After he left Ithaca, Rulloff went to New Jersey, where he worked in a factory. One night he dropped in on a revival meeting and soon the "strange brother" (little did they know how strange!) was asked to lead them in prayer, which he did, and then the clergy asked him to stay on and preach, which he did twice. Long after, he could say, "what a glorious old preacher I would have made!" Then he went to North Carolina to teach, but soon a letter from young Jarvis, who was in jail in Buffalo, called him north. He bribed a member or members of the grand jury, and Jarvis was released. They had a long talk, and Rulloff told Jarvis of his plan to write the great book on philology "which would sell for a large sum," and they seem to have worked out the terms of their partnership at that time. Jarvis would actively supply their income through crimes Rulloff would help him plan, and if plans went awry, he would use his wits and his legal training to get the impetuous Jarvis out of his jams. And the mutual dream was that this was temporary, for finally the great book would bring a fortune they would share. Before they could get to New York, Jarvis was again in trouble, this time caught with $1,600 worth of sewing silk. Jarvis seems to have specialized in stealing textiles and related materials and almost always (with one tragic exception) in western New York or New Jersey; the result of this was that neither of them was known to the New York police, though that was their base of operations for the next decade.

Rulloff himself was a bungling burglar; this may have been due to his limp or more likely to his compulsion for getting caught; in any event, Jarvis did better when he worked alone or with some other partner. In 1861 a Dutchess County caper of theirs failed, and while Jarvis escaped, Rulloff was sent to Sing Sing for two and a half years until May of 1864. While there he met an oafish fellow, ignorant and stupid, named William Dexter, also known as Davenport. They both worked in the cabinet shop, Rulloff as bookkeeper where his calligraphy delighted his keepers. After they were released Dexter joined Jarvis to make a trio of reasonably successful petty sneak thieves. During the Civil War, however, Jarvis was making his living joining the army, collecting his bounty, deserting only to enlist again under another name, and collecting another bounty. If the war had not come to a close, he would have been shot as a deserter, but luck was with him for the time being. He had banked some of the bounty money for Rulloff, when he would be free.

Much of the time during those years he and Jarvis were living in rented rooms owned by respectable people, spending much of their time studying or he was writing on his *magnum opus*, with a quiet game of euchre now and then; what little drinking they did was very mild, never any carousing, nothing out of the way for these model tenants. In 1869 they moved into two rooms in the home of Mr. and Mrs. Conrad Jacobs at 170 Third Avenue. Jarvis or both of them would go off now and then, be gone a few days or a week, and come home with some money to tide them over. But Professor Leuri was coming closer and closer to his great triumph when the scholarly world would hail this great discoverer, this Columbus, this Leif Ericson of philology, this Magellan of the beginnings of language.

So it was that he went to Vassar and the American Philological Association, and so it was that he came home defeated for the moment but still convinced that his genius and his overwhelming contribution could not long go unrecognized. Life went on as it had: he worked at his books, honing his arguments, finding more and more "proof." Jarvis and Dexter did a job here and there, one in a dry goods store owned by D. M. and E. G. Halbert on the north side of Court Street, between Water St. and the Chenango River in Binghamton, New York. The months passed, a year passed, and in the middle of August 1870, the trio took the Erie Railroad to Binghamton, not far from Ithaca and Cayuga Lake, not far from Dryden and Lansing, not quite far enough.

Halbert's store, as Jarvis and Dexter very well knew, was having a wing added to its rear, leaving the basement area easily accessible. A confederate had kept them informed, and he met them in Binghamton, but he had failed to tell them that a circus was in town when they arrived at five o'clock, the afternoon of August 15. The two younger men were to do all the work; Rulloff "was only to be a passenger." They had a small satchel, an umbrella, and a good sized traveling bag in which to carry home the loot. They had brought an appropriate set of tools, masks for each of them, and chloroform, for they knew that on the first floor two young men hired to guard the place would be sleeping, Frederick A. Mirick and Gilbert S. Burrows. All three robbers were armed with pistols, negating Rulloff's contention that he had not expected to play an active role. They hid out that night and most of the next day. The circus crowds had disrupted their original plans, and there was much backing and filling while Jarvis made up his mind as what to do and when. They had tied a boat in the Chenango River close to the rear of the store so they could escape afterward; this was the same procedure they had used in June. By one o'clock in the morning of August 17, they were ready, and Dexter bored a hole in the temporary door in the back of the cellar, and they were soon inside. Rulloff stayed downstairs while his protegés went to work. Jarvis put chloroform over the faces of the guards. The gaslight at the head of the stairs was enough for them to pick out the most expensive silks, and Rulloff joined them. They wrapped up the best silks, and Jarvis took an armful down to the cellar. Rulloff was standing at the foot of the bed whispering quietly to Dexter when Jarvis fell over something in the cellar, making considerable noise. Mirick woke up, grabbed his pistol, pointed it at Rulloff, and pulled the trigger four times, to no effect for the pistol failed to go off. Then Mirick lunged at Rulloff, who fled down the stairs, and Mirick threw the seat of a customer's stool at him, hitting him on the head. Meanwhile Burrows was grappling with Dexter and had got him down. Rulloff told Jarvis they had better leave, but Jarvis refused to leave Dexter. They waited a moment, then heard Dexter cry out, so they rushed upstairs to find him on the floor held down by Burrows, being hit by Mirick with an iron box opener. Jarvis fired into the air to frighten them off. Burrows went over near the bed, whereupon Mirick went after Jarvis, bent him back over a counter with one hand while he caught him painfully by the privates with the other. Rulloff came up behind Mirick and shot him twice through the head, killing him instantly.

The trio headed for the river together, Rulloff supporting the other two. They forgot about the boat, and Jarvis said they could easily ford the river as it was only a few inches deep. But he failed to reckon with a deep hole in the river bed, and first Dexter then Jarvis disappeared into the Chenango not to reappear. Rulloff was suddenly totally alone and penniless.

Meanwhile Burrows had aroused the town, and a fire bell was rung. Almost immediately the streets were full of excited citizens. Wandering around, Rulloff had a hard time finding the tree where they had left their bags. He had taken off his patent leather Oxfords so as to make no sound in Halbert's, now he stuffed some papers in the toe of one of Jarvis' boots and put them on. He went to the railroad yards hoping to grab a ride on a freight train, but just as he saw a train coming he was accosted by deputies. Moving fast, he ducked in front of the engine and ran off, eluding his enemies. He hid in a privy he found near the railroad yard, but what he didn't know was that the owner, who had heard the ruckus, was sitting on his back porch, pistol in hand thinking someone wanted to steal his fruit. Sitting there, smoking for an hour or so, the man began to think someone was hiding inside the privy. He silently approached the little building to find Rulloff cowering in a corner; pistol in hand the man turned him over to the police.

Rulloff said he had been visiting in Union, a few miles away, had missed his train, and hoped to visit other friends a few miles east. He was respectably dressed, and no one seemed to notice his wet pants leg. Burrows was not sure he could identify him, but on a chance they held him in jail. Friday morning the bodies of Jarvis and Dexter were found close by the abutment of a bridge. There was plenty of evidence to connect them with the murder, but when their bloated bodies were shown to Rulloff, without so much as a gasp of surprise he declared he had never seen either of them before. Later he went through a long questioning and survived it very well. Just as he was about to be released a Judge Balcom, before whom he had once argued a writ of *habeas corpus*, entered the room and recognized him. Yes, allowed Rulloff, that was right, and it explained all his actions. Having been given a bad name in those parts because of his earlier misfortunes, he did not want to be identified. So the coroner and the district attorney apologized for keeping him, and he went on his way.

Then somebody put two facts together. One of the Oxford shoes they found in Halbert's basement had a depression where the owner presumably lacked a great toe. And hadn't Rulloff lost a toe or two in his time? So they ran after him and brought him back and clapped him in irons.

It was a long, slow process by which the New York police gradually put together the relationship between Jarvis, Dexter, and Rulloff. Their avoidance of New York criminals, their endless aliases, the seeming respectability of Rulloff and the attractive Jarvis, and the lack of clues delayed procedures considerably, but piece by piece the puzzle was solved. Finally the Jacobs were confronted with the fact that Professor Leurio, that learned, charming old scholar, was a murderer, not once but several times.

The trial for the murder of Mirick attracted great attention, and every day crowds gathered hours before the court opened, everyone hoping to get a seat. That a large preponderance of these people were women surprised journalists of the time, who invariably thought it odd that "ladies"—and these obviously were "ladies"—wanted to see and hear the drama, most especially wanted to see this strangely attractive, repulsive man. The nineteenth-century journalists seemingly could never separate the gossamer dream girl from flesh and blood woman with drives and a curiosity of her own, for at almost every murder trial they comment on what seemed to them a contradictory mystery.

The prosecution piled up evidence beyond contradiction: the long relationship of the three burglars, the peeling away of aliases, the tools of the professional thief found in Rulloff's rooms, the lost toe (or toes) and the telltale shoes, the evidence of Burrows recounting his night of horror. At one point when Rulloff, who insisted on taking an aggressive part in the trial, asked Burrows, "How much light was there in the store?" Burrows replied, "Well, I can't say. You know how much light there was." A loud applause from the audience was one of the rare breaks in decorum throughout the trial.

The defense was very simple and very fragile. It sought to reduce the degree of the crime by showing that the unnecessary violence of Mirick and Burrows had provoked the murder. It was argued that persons in their position were only justified in using violence as would secure the robbers, no more. No untampered jury in upstate New York under the given circumstances would have bought that argument.

So on January 12, 1871, the jury retired a little before noon and returned six hours later. The verdict was "guilty as charged," and the next day Rulloff was ordered to be hanged from the neck until dead. The case went up to the Court of Appeals, but in no way was the trial invalidated. Finally the terminal date was set for May 18, 1871.

His weeks in prison were devoted, in so far as possible, to his "philological discovery." He saw practically no one but made an exception when he learned that R.H. Mather, a pro-

fessor of Greek at Amherst, wanted to meet him. Mather went
to the cell, "a long narrow granite-built room, but high and
furnished with plenty of light and pure air." Rulloff asked him
very politely if he could remain long enough to learn something
of the beauties of his theory of language and when the professor
agreed, "with the most winning courtesy" Rulloff offered him a
chair. Mather told him that he had once seen a critique Rulloff
had written while in Auburn Prison of Tayler Lewis' edition of
Plato's *Dialogues* and he wanted to know how he had learned
Greek. The smiling answer came that it was by the most honest
work—he had never been to college or university. Then, to
show his learning he had Mather select passages from Greek literature which he then recited from memory: Socrates *Memorabilia* 3d chapter, 1st book, from *The Iliad* and Sophocles "then,"
continued Mather, "in order to show his thoroughness, he criti-
cised the common rendering of certain passages and he did it
with such subtlety and discrimination and elegance as to show
his critical study of these nicer points was more remarkable
than his powers of memory. Subtlety of analysis and of reason-
ing was the marked characteristic of his mind."

That Rulloff had a most unusual mind is undeniable; he
dabbled in medicine, the law, pharmacology, archeology,
conchology, entymology, design, wood carving, phrenology,
and chemistry. His power to charm and his violent temper balanced each other. The only person for whom he seems to have
cared for any length of time was Jarvis, but he could look on his
bloated corpse without showing the slightest emotion. Monu-
mental though his crimes were, yet he lacked the finesse, the superb accomplishments of a master criminal.

The last days of Edward Rulloff were interrupted frequently by reporters looking for a new angle and by clergymen
hoping to convert a declared atheist. He would talk to anyone
who wanted to hear his theories of linguistics but avoided any
talk of his crimes. He wanted no prayers or clergymen at his
hanging, and once when a priest held up a crucifix, Rulloff
yelled at him, "Take that damned thing away." Mixed with all
this was that swollen ego and self pity. To a reporter who discussed his theory of language with him he said, "I have done

that which will make this epoch illustrious to other generations, but I go to my grave unrecognized and unrewarded." And I think he believed every word of it.

The hanging on May 18, 1871, was uneventful except that his hands were in his pockets when he was jerked into eternity, and one of his hands flew out and in his last moments he put it back in his pocket. They amputated his head to examine the brain, which weighed fifty-nine ounces, five ounces less than Daniel Webster's and is still to be seen at Cornell.

In central New York Rulloff's name is alive in the local folklore. My late friend Ed Barron who grew up in Lansing used to explore "Rulloff's Cave" where he was supposed to have hidden his wife's body. Local historical societies have photographs of him and his cronies, a piece of the hang rope and other memorabilia, but Rulloff's manuscript is missing, and sadly no one ever teaches his theory of the formation of language at Cornell or anywhere else, but then what can you expect in a world so full of humbugs?

Folk Art

I NCREASINGLY since 1949 my scholarly interests have centered on American folk art. The year of research, from Quebec to Texas, under a grant from the National Endowment for the Humanities opened our eyes to the wonderful range and variety, the creativity, the artistic boldness of the artists who were not trained as artists. I think it was about 1968 that I began to offer at the Cooperstown Graduate Program a course in American folk art; since 1973 Agnes Halsey Jones has team-taught with me.

"The Triumph of American Folk Art" appeared in *Search*, a publication of the State University of New York, in the last issue before it folded, Fall 1978. The article has been shortened considerably, throwing the emphasis on the Cooperstown collection.

The other two pieces relate to the Bicentennial, that birthday party that turned out so much better than most of us expected. "Genre in American Folk Art" was written for a symposium held by the Friends of Independence National Historical Park in Philadelphia and later published by them under the editorship of John C. Milley as *Papers on American Art*, 1976. "Outward Signs of Inner Beliefs: Symbols of American Patriotism" was the introduction to the catalog of the special Bicentennial exhibit of the New York State Historical Association in 1976. The subject had been of considerable interest to me ever since we acquired the painted window shade of "Washington and Liberty" from the Nadelman collection, as an article I wrote for *Antiques* in 1958 would show; it was called "Liberty and Considerable License."

I have twice in these papers leaned heavily on the research of former students: the best survey of the history of the folk art movement is Beatrix Rumford's "Uncommon Art of the Common People: A Review of Trends in the Collecting and Exhibiting of American Folk Art" which will be found in *Perspectives on American Folk Art*, edited by Ian M. G. Quimby and Scott T. Swank, 1980. And the basic research on the Van Bergen Overmantle was done by Kristin Gibbons for her masters' thesis in the Cooperstown Graduate Program, SUNY Oneonta, in 1965. Of course no one would ever have heard of the Van Bergen Overmantle if Mable Smith, historian of Greene County, had not found it and pointed us toward it.

The Triumph of
American Folk Art

AMERICAN folk art has burst into significance. Those modest artifacts made by ordinary, often uneducated people — from weathervanes and quilts to figureheads and paintings — have come into their own.

The evidence is all around us. New York, Georgia, Ohio, Michigan, and Pennsylvania have all had major shows of the folk art of their states; and folk life centers are cropping up north and south. Since the influential exhibit, "The Flowering of American Folk Art," at New York City's Whitney Museum in 1974, there has been an explosion of books, television programs, and seminars on people's art, as well as a new appreciation by conservative art critics and a broad new public.

At the national level Congress has established a Folk Life Center. The Smithsonian Institution has held annual folk festivals. And the National Endowments are paying increased attention to research and exhibits in folk arts and crafts.

The movement seems to be tugging us into new views of human nature and the place of art in our lives. We explore the possibility that men and women are natural aesthetes, decorators, and picture makers as much as they are natural hunters, food gatherers, and tool makers. Art, we are coming to realize, is much more than the fine arts. In New York the Museum of

Natural History recently mounted a major exhibit of the extraordinary art of prehistoric man, trumpeting the fact that people were creating pictorial art in caves at the same time that they were chipping stones into spearheads to fight the woolly mammoth.

While the American folk art phenomenon may seem like a sudden volcanic eruption, it has actually been fifty years in coming. The history of that rise from total obscurity to an increasingly prominent place in our nation's heritage provides a revealing glimpse of how American sensibilities can be refined and reshaped and by whom.

Interest in American folk art seems to have begun in Maine in the early 1920s. An artist and writer named Hamilton Easter Field, who ran the Ogunquit School of Painting and Sculpture each summer, used to rent fishing shacks to the young artists who studied there. To furnish these shacks he scoured the antique shops and went to the auctions around Ogunquit, Maine; and he brought back homemade rugs and bed covers, unsophisticated paintings and carvings, weathervanes, and decoys.

Among the artists who came to Ogunquit at the time were some people now significant in the history of American art: Marsden Hartley, William Zorach, Bernard Karfiol, and Robert Laurent, to name a few. Several of them admired the decorations that Field had collected for their shacks and began collecting similar objects for their own studios and homes. Back in New York other artists saw these simple, pleasant designs and began to collect for themselves. Among these were the painter Charles Sheeler and the sculptor Elie Nadelman. Nadelman especially caught the fever and collected extensively.

These artists understood the aesthetic values of these earlier, untrained artists and the solutions they inherited or invented to deal with color, perspective, modeling, composition, and abstraction. They were fascinated by the strong sense of design, frequently employed at the expense of realism; and they were captivated by the joining of art and function in such works as decoys, pictorial hooked rugs, or patchwork quilts. Some of these artists saw the folk artists as precursors of their own art, which was responsive to the turbulent movements of the 1920s.

In 1926 the group at Ogunquit was joined by a young man

John Worf. Like the parents of today who take rolls of photographs of their children, so the parents of earlier times turned to the available artists to record the young. John's siblings were painted at the same time by the same artist in that artistic flowering after the Revolution. Anonymous, oil on canvas, 23¾" x 16⅝", 1784, reproduced through the courtesy of the New York State Historical Association, Cooperstown.

Afro-Indian Cigar Store Figure. Tradition tells us that this very early trade sign was the work of a slave named Job in Freehold, New Jersey. The fringe, the moccasins, the bunches of cigars are elements that continued, but the West African head and shoulders, the masklike face are unique. "Job," polychromed wood, 4′11″, c. 1800, reproduced through the courtesy of the New York State Historical Association, Cooperstown.

Cigar Store Indian. Julius Melcher was no primitive carver but a Paris-trained wood sculptor of extraordinary skills. A careful student of Indians at first hand, his figures exhibit an elegance and authenticity unequaled by his contemporaries. Julius Melcher, (signed "M") poly-chromed wood, 73″ high, 1875–1900, reproduced through the courtesy of the New York State Historical Association, Cooperstown.

named Holger Cahill, a thoughtful, scholarly man, highly creative and orderly in his thinking. He had spent the previous summer studying peasant arts in northern Europe and Scandinavia. He brought to a collection like that of Robert Laurent a perspective that included not only his own discerning eye but also an unusual historical awareness of the long tradition of European folk art.

By 1930 Holger Cahill had fulfilled a dream of the late John Cotton Dana, the innovative leader of the Newark Museum in New Jersey, by staging the first major show of the art of "American Primitives," as they were called. The Newark Museum was not only one of the most forward-looking of the time but a significant center of American art. Cahill exhibited eighty-three paintings—portraits, landscapes, and decorative pictures—pieces he gathered up from the private collections of his artist friends and others and from the museum's own collection. Late the next year, 1931, he put together another show there of three-dimension objects: ships' figureheads, decoys, cigar store sculpture, weathervanes, and the like. This show he called "American Folk Sculpture."

The shows created such a stir that the new, avant-garde Museum of Modern Art in New York City asked Cahill to mount an exhibit for them, which he did in 1932. That show had 173 items, of both paintings and sculpture, and it marked the arrival of folk art on the major art scene in New York. With one exception all these anonymously loaned objects were from the collection of Abby Aldrich Rockefeller (Mrs. John D. Rockefeller, Jr.) and in time became the nucleus of the collection at Colonial Williamsburg which bears her name.

What was of almost equal importance with the 1930–32 shows were Holger Cahill's catalogs to accompany them. In these he explained what folk art is and established definitions and limits which, with only minor disagreements, are still valid today. He wrote in his *American Folk Art: The Art of the Common People, 1750–1900* for the Museum of Modern Art:

> Folk art . . . is the expression of the common people, made
> by them and intended for their use and enjoyment. It is not
> the expression of professional artists made for a small cul-

tured class, and it has little to do with the fashionable art of its period.

It does not come out of an academic tradition passed on by schools, but out of a craft tradition plus the personal quality of the rare craftsman who is an artist. Folk art . . . is the work of people with little book learning in art techniques and no academic training.

Among the older museums to build their own folk art collections was Fenimore House, the museum of the New York State Historical Association at Cooperstown. Because this has become the major collection in New York it might be worthwhile to take a look at how it began.

One day in 1949, Janet MacFarlane, then the curator, and I were in our Farmers' Museum. I picked up a barley fork, a beautiful, flowing rivulet of wood. Could we put together, I asked, from the collected items of The Farmers' Museum and Fenimore House a small room full of folk art? Miss MacFarlane thought we could, and we began to make a list.

That Saturday morning Stephen C. Clark, Sr., the chairman of our board, dropped by my office for our customary weekly chat. While his own collecting had been in American academic painting and the French impressionists (now at Yale and the Metropolitan), Mrs. Clark had made a small bijou collection of primitive watercolors and theorems for their summer home. As a trustee of the Museum of Modern Art (with Abby Aldrich Rockefeller), Stephen Clark had been acquainted with American folk art since Cahill's show there in 1932. We discussed what Janet MacFarlane and I had in mind, and he quickly saw it as an appropriate extension of the depiction of folk life to which The Farmers' Museum is dedicated.

A few days later Mr. Clark phoned, asking me to come to New York City. His friend Lincoln Kirsten, the promoter of American ballet, had told him that Mrs. Elie Nadelman, widow of the Polish-American sculptor, was selling some of the second collection of folk art she and her husband had made. (They had sold the first one to Manhattan's New-York Historical Society during the difficult times of the Depression.)

The Nadelman house, high over the Hudson at Riverdale,

That's My Doll. The pastels of this period seldom show action of any kind, and pictures of children are usually fairly static. These two are like youngsters we know. Anonymous, pastel on paper, 22½" x 30", c. 1805, reproduced through the courtesy of the New York State Historical Association, Cooperstown.

Francis O. Watts with Bird. John Brewster, Jr., the artist, despite the fact that he was a deaf mute, had a long and successful career as an itinerant painter, with special skills for depicting children. The tethered bird held by a child is a portrait cliché borrowed from upper class paintings. John Brewster, Jr., oil on canvas, 35¼″ x 36¼″, 1805, reproduced through the courtesy of the New York State Historical Association, Cooperstown.

Lady with a Nosegay. To date nothing is known of A. Ellis, but his work is characteristic of the painter who is artistically naive: the flatness of face and body, the linearity, the strongly repeated rhythms in the treatment of the hair, the collar, the details of the dress and belt. Signed A. Ellis, oil on panel, 26½" x 22⅛", c. 1830, reproduced through the courtesy of the New York State Historical Association, Cooperstown.

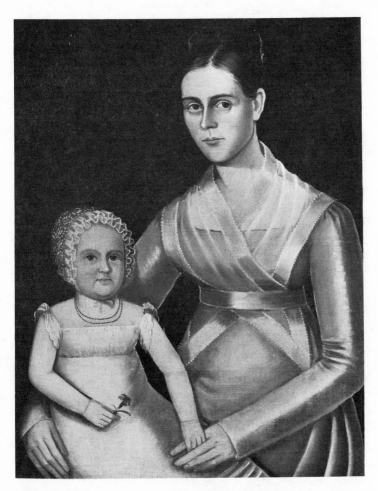

Mother and Child in White. Ammi Phillips has become one of the best known artists of this group. An itinerant working in the Hudson and Connecticut river valleys, he often succeeds, as he does here with the young mother, in conveying a sense of character and serenity. Babies are harder to paint. Ammi Phillips, oil on canvas, 33½" x 27¾", c. 1830, reproduced through the courtesy of the New York State Historical Association, Cooperstown.

was bulging with more folk art than I had ever seen. Mrs. Nadelman, Mr. Kirsten, and I stayed together while Mr. Clark wandered through the collection by himself. After a couple of hours he called me aside. "If you could have twelve pieces from this collection for our museum, which ones would you pick?" Nothing had prepared me for that, but I gulped and named twelve. There was a long silence, and then he said, "Well, I agree with you on eleven of them. Let's buy thirteen." So he did.

We converted the decaying swimming pool in the basement of Fenimore House into two new galleries, and we opened our first exhibit of folk art in the summer of 1949, combining the Nadelman acquisitions with pieces already in the museum. The Nadelman items remain among the most distinguished pieces in the collection, now a hundredfold larger.

Only a few months later, in the winter of 1949–50, the staff at the New York State Historical Association was working on the April 1950 special issue of *Art in America*, featuring the art of Fenimore House. The editor of *Art in America* was Jean Lipman, whose two books *American Primitive Painting* and *American Folk Art in Metal, Wood and Stone* were the first generously illustrated books in the folk art field and pioneering works. The summer before Mrs. Lipman had invited me to visit her and her husband at their home in Wilton, Connecticut. The house was a delight; every wall, every space was filled with folk art of all kinds. Just before the special issue of *Art in America* went to press, Stephen Clark, through the mediation of the dealer Mary Allis, bought the entire collection. We barely had time for a note in the magazine announcing this magnificent addition to our holdings. We created three more galleries adjacent to the old swimming pool to house it.

During the early 1950s the collection at Fenimore House continued to grow little by little. And then in 1958 Mary Allis came forward once more. A Mrs. William Gunn of Boston had just died and left a barn full of paintings which she had collected over the years but never viewed or enjoyed. Of the more than 500 works only a scant half dozen were in her house, and some of these were stacked in a closet. With rare speed Miss Allis had negotiated the sale of the whole lot to Mr. Clark, who had them transferred to a warehouse in New York. Through a

Stokes Coverlet. This rare example of an appliqued storytelling coverlet is comprised of chintzes and calicoes cut out of other pieces. The tree of life theme in the center is surrounded by scenes from everyday life. Hannah Stockton Stokes, various textiles, 91" x 103", c. 1830, reproduced through the courtesy of the New York State Historical Association, Cooperstown.

hot August Miss Allis, with occasional assists from Mr. Clark and me, winnowed the chaff from the wheat. About half were good to superb; the rest were dross. That summer I learned a lot about separating one from the other. The best came to our museum; Mary Allis disposed of the balance.

During these formative years, the New York State Historical Association's collection had the advantage of having as a trustee and adviser Nina Fletcher Little. Not only do she and her husband, Bertram K. Little, have what may be the most comprehensive collection of New England paintings and household arts in private hands but Mrs. Little is a scholar who, more than anyone else, has brought to light the biographical data of the eighteenth- and nineteenth-century portrait painters and their sitters. Her shrewd use of genealogical techniques, historical research, and broad knowledge of folk ways and customs have pushed back the curtains that kept us in the dark about the environment in which the nation's early folk artists worked. Museums with trustees of this calibre are as fortunate as they are rare.

By 1960 the collection at Fenimore House had a good representation of most categories of folk art, and in the 1970s examples of the work of twentieth-century folk artists such as Scholl, Edmondson, Wiener, and Tolson were added. Today it is one of the top-ranking collections in the country.

In 1964 the privately endowed New York State Historical Association joined forces with the State University of New York's College at Oneonta to form the Cooperstown Graduate Programs, offering masters' degrees in history museum studies and in American folk culture. The study of American folk art, appropriate to both of these programs, has been offered since 1968. Like other aspects of the two programs, the folk art study broke fresh academic ground. It had the tremendous advantage of a large, quality collection to work with at first hand, affording students the opportunity of practical and useful research projects. Many of the Cooperstown students have gone on to institute research in folk art at museums across the country.

Another source of strength at Cooperstown, both for teaching and research, is the archive of close to thirty thousand slides of folk art begun by Agnes Halsey Jones in 1972 when we had a grant from the National Endowment for the Humanities

Peaceable Kingdom. Edward Hicks painted this sermon more than a hundred times, usually including as he does here, a miniature detail of Benjamin West's *William Penn's Treaty with the Indians* and also borrowing from illustrated Bibles and religious publications. Edward Hicks, 30⅛" x 34½", 1840–45, reproduced through the courtesy of the New York State Historical Association, Cooperstown.

to sample folk art anywhere we chose. Since then she and our students have photographed, often in great detail, many of the major folk art shows. The archive has proved useful to scholars, museum curators, directors, and movie producers. The realism and detail of many folk paintings make them important historical documents. For instance, folk art can be a most useful source for the history of American clothing, folk architecture, farm and town layout, transportation, or everyday and holiday life.

All through the half century of American folk art's

Wisconsin Farm. Paul Seifert was a German-born artist who painted the farms of his Wisconsin neighbors. "People like my work, and I like to paint for them" summed up his attitude toward his work and audience. Paul A Seifert, watercolor, tempera, oil on cardboard, 15½" x 28", c. 1875, reproduced through the courtesy of the New York State Historical Association, Cooperstown.

growth, there have been two discordant notes. One concerns nomenclature, the other definition.

The word "folk" is a burr under some people's saddles. We all use the word "folks," as in "my folks" or "townsfolk," without embarrassment. But for some, the word "folk" is too reminiscent of an alien peasantry. They prefer terms like "naive art" or "primitive art" — even though "naive" seems an inappropriate word for skilled craftsmen and has patronizing overtones, and "primitive" connotes the stone age and crudity.

Then there is the question: what exactly is folk art? In 1950 Alice Winchester, the wise and scholarly editor of *Antiques*, asked thirteen collectors, museum administrators, and art historians to define folk art for her May issue. These distinguished ladies and gentlemen came to no consensus whatsoever. And there is still disagreement.

The fact is, however, that a body of paintings, carvings,

Col. Glover's Fishermen Leaving Marblehead for Cambridge, 1775.
J. O. J. Frost's early life was spent at sea as a Marblehead fisherman, but
after his marriage he operated a small restaurant. He was an enthusiastic local historian, and his paintings were history lessons for the young.
J. O. J. Frost, oil on wallboard, 23½" x 49½", 1920s, reproduced
through the courtesy of the New York State Historical Association,
Cooperstown.

needlework, and metal work exists which is not part of the fine
arts tradition (although sometimes it has been influenced by it).
Some of the folk artists were craftsmen with an aesthetic turn of
mind; some were amateurs who learned various skills in sec-
ondary school; some were self-taught professionals. While their
work lacks many of the qualities which give us pleasure in the
fine arts, it has other qualities which please: a directness of
statement, a vigor and originality, a boldness in the use of color,
a strong emphasis on rhythms and design.

Some of what we call American folk art comes from a long
handicraft tradition in fairly isolated or restrictive societies:
scrimshaw, Pennsylvania German and Swiss religious watercolors known as fraktur, quilts, Hispanic santos, gravestones,
small wooden carvings, the early hand-fashioned trade signs,
weathervanes, and ship carvings. There is general agreement
that under any definition this is folk art.

Problems arise, however, over such items as factory-made
weathervanes, trade signs which come off an assembly line

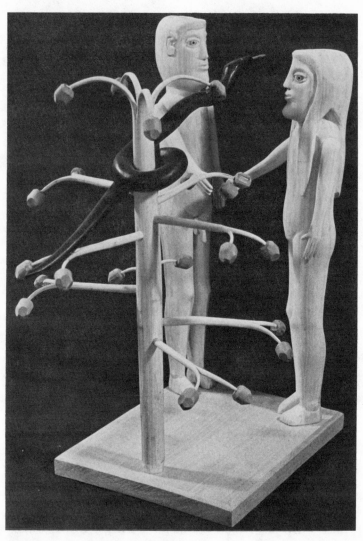

Adam and Eve: Temptation. Edgar Tolson, hard-drinking mountain preacher, farmer, carver has whittled scores of scenes from the Garden of Eden story. The stiff, uncomplicated figures evoke a surprising emotional response from viewers. Edgar Tolson, wood, 15″ high, 1960s, reproduced through the courtesy of the New York State Historical Association, Cooperstown.

Mary's Star. This purely decorative celebration is a characteristic example of the work of John Scholl, a German-born house carpenter in the Pennsylvania village of Germania. The scrolls, brackets, nails, and wooden balls are miniature versions of the decorations he made for houses. The bright colors of his paints make for a very lively result. John Scholl, wood, 68″ x 22⁵⁄₁₆″, 1907–1916, reproduced through the courtesy of the New York State Historical Association, Cooperstown.

(e.g., the later wooden Indians), school-taught arts such as the-orems, memorials, calligraphy, landscapes after prints, and portraits which show an acquaintance with academic portrai-ture, all of which have been called folk art for fifty years. The fact is that neither dealers, nor museums, nor collectors, nor magazine writers, nor the general public have made a distinc-tion between the two groups; they have lumped it all together and called it American folk art. And it is, I think, too late to change.

Some scholars in the growing field of American folk life who are concerned with traditional culture as a whole find this lack of definition and the loose use of the word "folk" confus-ing, not to say deplorable. They are concerned primarily with the environment from which the work comes, the patterns of culture handed down from generation to generation, and the viewpoint of the artist who created the object. As one of the ablest of their number is quoted as saying, "If you can't tell me who made it, I can't say whether it is folk art or not." At the op-posite pole are the collectors and dealers who have little interest in the authorship or history of an object but are concerned prin-cipally with the aesthetic qualities.

All of these contenders are like blind men stroking their elephant. What is needed is to see the beast in its entirety, to see the object in both its historical and cultural perspective, and to appreciate its aesthetic impact.

Whatever the disagreements and despite a whole range of research that still needs to be done, the relatively new field of American folk art has come of age. We have uncovered that buried stratum of our nation's art done by men, women, and adolescents who knew little of the art schools, dealers, or muse-ums. The work of these unsophisticated artists was created to bring enjoyment, to brighten life, to lift the heart out of its dreariness with pleasing lines and rhythms, bright colors, and attractive forms. The pleasure it sought to give, it still gives — as all true art must.

Genre in American Folk Art

I
N discussing American folk genre paintings, it may be useful if I define the term as I intend to use it. By "genre" I
mean a depiction of everyday life, a moment, an incident
involving human beings usually at a social level below that of
the more favored class. It is strong in specific detail and sharply
focused minutiae. "Folk" is used here to indicate the artist's un-
awareness of the fine points of academic painting, his artistic
naivete. But it also implies a cultural sympathy with the subject
matter, the artist usually belonging to the same class as the people in his picture, and painting experiences with which he is totally familiar.

The importance of a particular folk genre piece may be
greater as a document than as a work of art, and it should be
recognized as a supplement to the written word, as a historical
source. All social history is weak when it comes to the habits,
work, dress, attitudes, play, and religious life of the lower
classes in *any* society, and this is very true of Americans. People
who work with their hands keep few diaries, write few letters,
and until recently have seldom been a subject of concern to the
scholar. The genre painter captures such people as would a
modern photographer, a Cartier-Bresson, an Evans or Bourke-
White.

These are paintings which reflect a specific time and
place and, more often than not, the people depicted are ac-
quaintances of the artist. It is not an *idea* of a dance, nor an

167

ideal dance, that the artist shows us, but a dance which he attended and with people he knows. The naive artist's lack of discipline in composition and his tendency to "get it all in" leads to the inclusion of details a more sophisticated painter might well reject. Our man includes all the facts he knows to be part of the scene.

Compared with other types of naive painting — portraits, landscapes, or schoolgirl art — the genres comprise a relatively small percentage of the whole. This is particularly interesting in view of the great popularity of academic genres from 1820 to 1880 and the success of Currier and Ives and other print makers in selling genre subjects. The explanation may be that the folk artist lives within his own world and in most instances is unaware of or unconcerned with what the academic artists of his time are up to. On the other hand, the popularity and cheapness of lithographs may have discouraged the folk painters from entering the field. A few paintings may have been based on prints — *The Quilting Party* is a well known example — but I have found relatively few print sources for the approximately two hundred folk genres with which I am familiar. It is possible, of course, that many more of these paintings once existed but have been destroyed or lost.

It might be useful to compare briefly the academic and folk artists. In doing so, we recall that the roots of academic genre painting in this country go back ultimately to the seventeenth century Dutch masters but more immediately to Hogarth, Wilkie, and Greuze. Two important immediate factors in the nineteenth century were, first the climate of opinion in the Jacksonian period, with its egalitarian emphasis, making working people appropriate subjects for the artist and, second, the existence of the Dusseldorf School in Germany where many Americans studied, whence they brought home a slick and dramatic technique. They also brought back a tendency to think of the people in their paintings as beneath them socially and of the artist as a man apart.

As Patricia Hills has pointed out, favorite themes of the academic painter were tavern scenes, itinerant peddlers and musicians, the black man on the periphery of the action, with emphasis on gesture, anecdotal elements, moralizing and humor. Moreover, she concludes that "most scenes of everyday life in America were synthetic constructions, reflecting the cultural ideals and social myths of the picture producers and picture consumers — the painters' America — rather than the actual social circumstances of the majority of the people." While I think one could find many exceptions to this generalization, it stands as an important observation. Certainly the academic artists were painting pictures for a living and painting what well-to-do patrons would buy. They were deeply involved in painterly problems, the "how" more than the "what." They had artistic standards to meet, and many of them met those standards very well indeed.

In contrast to this, in many ways the folk genre artists present a very different profile. Judging from those on whom we have some biographical data, they were seldom earning their living pirmarily from their art; they were workers or craftsmen or housewives who painted as a sideline, seriously but only semi-professionally. They were personally close to the subject matter they painted, the work and play of kith and kin. There is no difference between artist and subject because they are of the same class, the same world. Often these paintings were not for sale but were for family or friends which meant there was no problem of pleasing a patron or gallery owner. Thus the three factors — artist, subject, ultimate owner, were all from the same level of society, the same community of interests and values. Herein lies a major difference between the folk and academic genre painting. There are also differences of mood. The folk artist is almost never sentimental; his work has little emotional vibration of any kind. Rather, it is clear eyed, factual, without moralizing. It often recounts an experience, seen rather than imagined, a scene frequently experienced over and over again. It is good humored but seldom comic; it causes a smile but never a guffaw.

Finally, it is evident that the folk artist is a good reporter; he creates a document as reliable as most diaries or reminiscences. When we are in a position to check out the painting with the available facts, repeatedly we find that the two jibe. The meticulous reporting of detail reflects an observing eye and a sure memory, producing a clean-cut statement. And this had to be so, if the community for which it was painted was to approve, for the folk may not know the fine points of painterliness, but they know how a harness is made and how it is fastened to a horse, how a flax scutch is used, how a street vendor's cart is painted. For such a public the *details* must be right; the perspective be damned. It is the facts that count just as they demanded an accurate likeness, above all else, in their portraits.

The genre topics covered by the folk artists would seem to fall in five general categories, one of them being *miscellaneous*, where only one or two examples are known to exist. A large grouping could be called *fun and games*, where we see dances, quilting and other bees, various summer and winter sports, hunting, eating, and the celebration of the holidays. The mood here is gay and the artists enter into the sense of fun. Another large group concerns the *work*. The most frequent are scenes of men involved in one or another aspect of agriculture, but lumbering, black smithing, and whaling are all represented. Women artists especially record the labors of women, both indoors and out, again reflecting the tendency of these painters to paint what they knew at firsthand. A small body of genres is concerned with the *rites of passage*, baptisms, courtship, weddings, funerals. I know of only two academic genre of weddings (Woodville and Krimmel) and only one funeral (Antrobus). The latter is a fairly popular subject with the folk artists, and there exists a handful of wedding pictures. The last grouping I have called *street scenes* to include parades, fires, militia, politicking, vending, and children at play. Here we get an extremely interesting insight to the everyday passing scene, its variety and colorful pleasures. The predominate mood of these paintings is cheerful and characterized by a gently amused acceptance of life as it is and no suggestion that it ought to be otherwise.

Only a handful of American genre paintings of any kind have survived from the eighteenth century, but two of the most significant are well within the definition of folk genre, the Van Bergen Overmantle and *The Old Plantation*.

The Van Bergen Overmantle, now attributed to John Heaton, was painted about 1733 on the farm of Marten Van Bergen; it is one of the earliest American landscapes (those are

the Catskill Mountains in the background, accurately recorded):
it is our earliest conversation piece and our earliest genre. I
would like to test it for its reliability as a document.

The first school of American portraiture developed in the
Hudson Valley between 1700 and 1750. Several score portraits
of members of the Dutch Hudson Valley families were painted,
but only the portraits have survived from the brushes of these
artists, artists of talents but in a limner, rather than academic,
tradition. Only portraits, *except* for a group of religious paintings and this scene created to be enjoyed over the mantle piece
of the home one sees depicted. It remained in that house until it
was demolished; thereafter the painting remained in the house
which replaced it, until the New York State Historical Association at Cooperstown bought it.

Here we see three adult and nine junior members of the
Van Bergen family, four black slaves, two white servants—quite
probably indentured—and two Catskill or Esopus Indians.
Part of the rarity of this piece lies in the representation of slaves
and servants in their working clothes and at their chores; also, I
know of no other eighteenth-century paintings of Hudson Valley Indians. There is also a catalog of livestock: horses, cows,
sheep, chickens, dogs. We shall want to consider the architectural evidence for houses, barn, and out buildings.

We might start with the fence, bull strong, pig tight and
sheep high, and the gate with its cross bar and finnealed posts.
In a contemporary portrait of an Albany miller, Abraham Wen-
dell (owned by the Albany Institute of History and Art), we see
corroboration of this detail when we look closely at the fence
enclosing his property. A farm wagon stands before his mill,
identical with the one in the Van Bergen painting, and similar
examples are to be found in the Enkheisen Museum in the Neth-
erlands, dating from the eighteenth century.

There exist interesting parallels to the hay barracks and
barn. The Roosevelt Library, for example, has a 1792 drawing
of a log barn with out buildings, drawn by P. Lodet in Mini-
sink, New York, which not only shows a hay barrack but indicates how the roof and floors can be raised and lowered to protect the hay. Agnes Halsey Jones has photographed a similar
structure in modern Holland. The barn is typical of the three-

Van Bergen Overmantle. This scene, painted on two boards nailed together was installed above the fireplace, first in the house it illustrates
and then in the house which replaced the original. Attributed to John

aisled Dutch barns, some two hundred of which still stand in
New York State. One which fell down only in the last few years
stood on the farm of Marten's brother Garrit and was identical
with the one in the painting.

Like many of the early houses in the foothills of the Catskills the Van Bergen's was of stone with a tile roof over the main
structure and shingles over the kitchen wing. Notice the little
dormers, the wooden gutter, the characteristic front stoop, the
double windows with solid, painted wooden blinds. One could
document this with mid-nineteenth-century photographs of
other Hudson Valley houses; on the other hand, we have photographed an almost identical farm house in southern Holland
with an almost identical barn, showing the prototypes our
people brought over with them as ideas of what a farm should
look like.

After seventy years of English domination, the Dutch in
New York dressed like Englishmen, and Mr. and Mrs. Van Bergen might be an English country squire and his lady; he is
shown in the stance affected by many men of his time when
having their portraits painted. There were seven children in the
family, all of whose names and dates we know. The three sons
are horsemen, or at least two of them are. Their four younger

Heaton, oil on wood, 18½″ x 88″, c. 1733, reproduced through the
courtesy of the New York State Historical Association, Cooperstown.

sisters assume little ladylike poses. The man and two boys coming from the right are presumably Garrit Van Bergen and two
of his sons accompanied by two dogs. One of these sons had his
portrait painted at the time of his marriage, and it is interesting
to note that he is shown with the same breed of pet.

Finally, the four slaves. We know that Mrs. Van Bergen received a slave as a wedding present from her father, and one
wonders if the elderly figure sitting down is that woman. The
others are younger and busy with their chores. It is worth noting as we observe the Esopus Indians that the man's dog is of a
very different lineage than the Van Bergen's. The two white
servants are probably indentured, and the vehicle loaded with
bags may well be carrying grain, for Van Bergen was part
owner of a grist mill.

The point I am hoping to make here is that these naive
painters with whom we are concerned can be very reliable reporters, worthy of the historian's attention and as credible as
the writers of letters and memoirs.

The Old Plantation, dated in the late 1790s on the basis of
its watermark and costumes, provides a rare insight to the survival of African cultural patterns in the South. From a variety
of newly evaluated sources we begin to see how much of Africa

The Old Plantation. This great anonymous document shows a score of
ways in which patterns imported from Africa were alive and active at
the close of the eighteenth century. Anonymous, watercolor on paper,
11¾" x 17⅞", c. 1790s, reproduced through the courtesy of The Abby
Aldrich Rockefeller Folk Art Center.

survived in the New World. Here the use of the scarf and the
walking stick in the dance, the Yoruba head dresses of men and
women, the musical instruments (the jambar, ancestor of the
guitar; the gudu gudu or drum made by stretching an animal
skin to form the drum head; the bottles or jugs containing
drinks for the musicians) all indicate strong memories of native
traditions the blacks had by no means left behind. The highly
individualized portraits of the men and women with a complete avoidance of stereotyping, is worthy of special note. They
raise the possibility that this is the work of a black artist. As early
as 1773 there were slaves in Charleston specifically trained as
artists (see advertisements reproduced in Sidney Kaplan's *The
Black Presence in the Era of the American Revolution*, Washington, D.C., 1973), and internal evidence points to a remarkable sympathy and familiarity with the black cultural patterns.

South Carolina, where this painting was found by Holger Cahill years ago, received its slaves directly from Africa with no
West Indian stopover, and African survivals are still more numerous there than anywhere else in the United States. Here is a
document worthy of the most careful analysis by the cultural
historians and the scholars in black history. It is also a watercolor that offers the delights of instinctively created rhythms of
form and color; in every way, it is a painting that dances.

The nineteenth century was of course the great flowering
time for all kinds of genre paintings. One is tempted to linger
over that Pennsylvania German carpenter, Lewis Miller, whose
pictorial record of the daily life in York, Pennsylvania, is so
amusingly descriptive. Part contemporary history, part autobi-
ography, his hundreds of watercolor sketches record myriad aspects of common experience, done with a chuckling humor.

Perhaps we can learn more from Lindon Park, the classic
example of folk genre painter. The late Professor Maurice Mook
had planned a biography and study of his work; one can only
hope that someone else will complete the task, for Park's *Flax
Scutching Bee* at the National Gallery is one of the masterpieces
of this whole group, indeed, one of the masterpieces of American folk art.

Lindon Park was born in 1826 into a Scotch-Irish family,
the youngest of nine children. His father was a surveyor in
western Pennsylvania and laid out the village of Marion Center.
He had a tan yard, a grist mill, and a cabinet shop where Lindon was apprenticed. At an early age the boy began a lifelong
refusal to eat meat, the first observed of many eccentricities.

As a lad he helped make "pup rafts" which later were
combined to create the great lumber rafts which went down
the West Branch of the Susquehanna each spring. He may have
taken short trips on these but was never a bona fide raftsman.
Rather he made furniture in the cabinet shop and painted signs
and carriages all his life.

When the Civil War came he did not enlist until 1864,
when he was thirty-eight years old. Stationed in Washington,
he was assigned to the burial corps and apparently did some
guard duty at the White House. As you might expect, his refusal to eat meat got him in trouble with the military estab-

Rafting. The last in a series of logging scenes by Lindon (or Linton) Park, it depicts a not unusual hazard in getting the great logging rafts down the Susquehanna. Lindon (or Linton) Park, oil on canvas, 23⅛″ x 35⅛″, c. 1874, reproduced through the courtesy of the New York State Historical Association, Cooperstown.

lishment, and he took the matter directly to the president.

Mr. Lincoln asked, "You want me to turn you out to graze like Nebuchadnezzer?"

"It would be better than salt pork."

So he was given a note saying, "The bearer, Lindon Park, is herewith granted permission to browse wherever he chooses. Signed A. Lincoln."

After the war he traveled a little then returned to Marion Center to remain the rest of his life. This began a period of inventions: a feather renovator for coverlets, a vegetable grinder, a ventilating (venetian) window blind which he patented in 1874 and for which he won a prize at the Centennial Exposition in 1876. Then a wall pocket and hat rack. "Nicest little thing made in Marion and only one man can make it," he advertised.

Flax Scutching Bee. This is the closest an American artist came to capturing the spirit of Breughel on the frontier, from the sober-sided to the rollicking, the ants to the grasshoppers, they are all here as one who was there remembered them forty years later. Lindon (or Linton Park), oil on canvas, 31¼" x 50¼", 1885, reproduced through the courtesy of the National Gallery of Art, Washington; Gift of Edgar William and Bernice Chrysler Garbisch.

Meanwhile he was painting wagons and signs, doing graining. A quiet man, generous, full of good humor, a bachelor living alone most of his life.

It is in the 1870s that his earliest paintings are dated; nine of his works are extant, and there are rumors of others, either extant or lost. Eight are genres including a group of logging scenes beginning with cutting and hauling logs, leaving the saw mill, the raft of logs beginning its journey and finally a breaking up of the raft as it hits a boulder in the river.

The National Gallery has three of Park's paintings, one of Merino sheep which the man who had commissioned it wouldn't accept because it had too much landscape and not enough sheep; then a rare example of a sentimental theme, called *Dying Tonight on the Old Camp Ground* painted for the GAR of which he was a devoted member, and finally the classic, *Flax Scutching Bee*.

Again, as in the Van Bergen Overmantle, we are given precise information about building construction, farm layout, hay stacks, flax processing from the dangers in roasting it, to the crushing of the outer husks on a flax brake, to the communal scutching or taking off the husks with wooden knives. But more important than the details of rural technology is the recording of moods and attitudes in frontier America. Park has created an American Breughel, and one's eye moves with delight from upright sobriety to amorous ribaldry, from wordly reality to gentle conversation, all this on a valley farm but recently cut from the wilderness.

The folk genre is by no means a lost art for our own times have seen some of the best examples in the work of Queena Stovall, Mario Sanchez, Clementine Hunter, and Ralph Fasanella. In the twenty-five decades since the Van Bergen Overmantle was painted our folk artists have been providing us with a remarkably useful, and often engaging and aesthetically satisfying, body of information about the ways our average citizens have lived, worked, played, and died. They have created a still neglected reservoir of information about the American people which calls for understanding and appreciation.

Symbols of
American Patriotism

NO one living in our times needs to be reminded of the vitality and importance of symbols to people all over the world. For two thousand years the cross has symbolized not only a religion but also a thousand points of view. Every time a new country joins the United Nations a new flag is raised on the plaza before the world's capitol. In the last few years we have seen long hair opposed to crew cuts; we have seen the peace symbol, or as its enemies called it "chicken tracks," counterpointed to the Stars and Stripes; we have seen the Star of David and the Crescent glaring at each other. We have seen the clenched fist; we have seen the Statue of Liberty and wedding rings. All these are symbols of important emotional values around which men's and women's lives have been woven. As the Bicentennial begins, it is appropriate that we look at the symbols which have represented this land and its people from its beginning as a few struggling communities along the seacoast to the present day. This exhibition surveys the symbols that have spoken of our pride and our hopes, our chauvinism and our bona fide love of country.

One of the earliest native symbols to appear on this continent, representing a government, was the Pine Tree Shilling issued in Massachusetts in 1652. This was an emblem related to one of the most universal of all symbols the "Tree of Life," — "Ever green, ever blooming, ever bearing," the opposite of the "Tree of Knowledge," in the garden of Eden. In 1652 Massa-

179

chusetts decreed that all of its money should carry the pine tree — "The Tree that never loses its leaves" — a symbol that was to continue actively down to the Revolution when American ships carried a flag with the pine tree on it with the words, "An appeal to heaven." And the pine tree becomes in time the Tree of Liberty, which Jefferson said "must be refreshed from time to time with the blood of patriots and tyrants."

The pine tree was not a universal symbol on the new continent. Perhaps the most frequently used symbol in those early years, while we were still separate colonies and ununited, was the American Indian warrior, the new man who not only stood for the red man but for his neighbor the colonist — his enemy, his sometime friend. These two were symbols which we adopted on this side of the Atlantic.

European engravers as early as the sixteenth century were picturing America as an Indian female, sometimes as the Indian Queen, sometimes as the younger Indian Princess. She stood side by side with three other females, Asia, Africa, and Europe. Often she derived details from the southern hemisphere and from Mexico, with great cornucopias filled with gold and jewels, with the feathered mantle and skirt of the Aztecs, with llamas and armadillos and other strange animals. She was voluptuous, rich, and vulnerable. Engravers in Holland, Germany, England, and France were presenting the New World in these terms. But as the eighteenth century moved forward a slightly different young Indian woman became the symbol for the thirteen American colonies. Sometimes she wore an Indian headdress and a skirt of feathers or tobacco leaves; later she sported a classical Grecian gown.

The Whigs in London were particularly active in adapting this symbol to their uses in cartoons. One of the best examples is a 1774 London engraving called *Liberty Triumphant or the Downfall of Oppression.* Here Britannia and the Genius of Britain discuss the Tory government, of which she says, "The conduct of those degenerate sons will break my heart." Our particular concern here is America herself wearing the headdress of an Indian, but by this time she is merging with another figure — a classical figure. The Sons of Liberty are dressed as Indians as they were at the Boston Tea Party, but they are not so

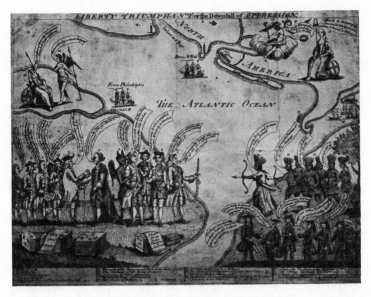

Liberty Triumphant or the Downfall of Oppression. America, dressed in a semiclassical gown but with Indian headdress, leads the Sons of Liberty against Lord Bute and his cohorts. Britannia and the Goddess of Liberty deplore the situation. Anonymous, engraving, 10″ x 14″, 1774, reproduced through the courtesy of Agnes Halsey Jones.

much Indians as they are the new man—the American. The cartoon was reproduced in this country and must have found an echo in many an American heart. The combination of the Indian costume and the classical costume was not immediate, as late as the 1780s America still sometimes appeared as a young Indian woman with feathered headdress and tobacco miniskirt. Eventually the Indian Princess lost her symbolic meaning, and while the female Indian remained a constant in America, she appeared mostly in cartouches and in the engravings of stock certificates. With the mass production of cigar store figures during the nineteenth century, she no longer had any particular symbolic significance. As a symbol for America she had been replaced by a totally classical lady.

This new figure was tall, full breasted, usually with flowing hair and a dress of classical design which fell to her ankles. She often wore Greek sandals. E. McClung Fleming has carefully denoted the characteristics that went with her differing nomenclature. Sometimes she is "America"; sometimes "Columbia"; sometimes "Liberty." But in a larger sense, she is the American ideal — the Genius of America; or, as Jefferson referred to her, a "Fine Female Figure." We see her in many forms on many objects; on coins and as ships figureheads, on ceramics and political banners, *ad infinitum*. She comes to us from a period when the founding fathers, steeped in classical traditions, were fondly aware of the classical rediscoveries of the seventeenth and eighteenth centuries and were determined to create a new Roman Republic — a new Greek democracy in the New World.

Two other symbols from classical iconography became important in this country long before the end of the eighteenth century. The liberty cap, which goes back to Greek and Roman times as a device worn by men freed from slavery, had strong English roots but certainly was impressed upon the popular consciousness by Hogarth's famous engravings of the Whigs' hero, John Wilkes, sitting cross-eyed and lecherous, holding a liberty cap on a liberty pole. The English cartoons and the French prints of the late eighteenth century frequently utilized this motif, which early became an accessory of the Fine Female Figure — sometimes placed on her head, in which case we are apt to think of her as Liberty; sometimes carried on a pole, or occasionally on top of a flag pole. In due time it was to appear on coins and seals, in cartoons, on chinaware, and sometimes carved in the round to carry in parades or to adorn wooden statues of the Fine Female Figure.

Another classical inheritance is the eagle which appeared occasionally before 1782 but really began to spread its wings after its adoption by the Congress as one element in the great seal in 1782. In Roman antiquity the eagle had been a symbol of Jove and so a symbol of power and majesty. A curious accident encouraged the widespread distribution of the combined symbol of the Fine Female Figure and the eagle. Originally it had no relation to the United States. In 1791 an English painter named William Hamilton painted an oval watercolor of Hebe offering a cup to the eagle (Jove), and this in due time was made into a print by the English engraver Facius. There is abundant evidence that this engraving was extremely popular in this country because so many of its derivatives have survived. Mrs. Trollope tells of a gentleman of culture in Cincinnati, famous for his critical tastes in the fine arts, who was shown a picture representing Hebe and the eagle sacred to Jupiter. He demanded in a satirical tone, "What is this?" "Hebe," came the reply. "Hebe?" sneered the man of taste, "What the devil has Hebe to do with the American eagle?" Certainly, in terms of the association that Americans were making between the young woman as a national symbol and the eagle, he was more right than Mrs. Trollope.

The eagle, like the liberty cap, became part of the American iconography at every level, on figureheads and tavern signs, on military insignia, in the fine and decorative arts.

In 1796 Edward Savage published an engraving of a now lost painting called *Liberty in the Form of the Goddess of Youth Giving Support to the Bald Eagle.* By this time Hamilton's Hebe has become an American, and while she is still the Goddess of Youth, she is by name, Liberty. "In the background," as he says in his description of the engraving, "is a monument supporting a flagstaff on which is suspended the cap of liberty and the union of the United States; in the offscape appears a view of Boston Harbor representing the evacuation of the British fleet. The Goddess of Liberty is supposed to be on Beacon Hill where she tramples under foot the key to the Bastille as the key of tyranny connected with the different orders of hereditary hostility." The key to the Bastille prison was a present sent by General Lafayette to George Washington, and it remains today at Mount Vernon as a symbol of the death of monarchial tyranny in France. Savage's engraving, like Hamilton's Hebe before it, must have been extremely popular, because when the untrained artists of this country looked around for a model on which to express their patriotism, over and over again they came back to Savage's *Liberty* as a source of stimulus, partly because it contained so many of the beloved and totally accepted symbols of the new land.

Eagle Figurehead. Probably carved for a small naval vessel, this bird has authority. Anonymous, wood, 21" long, 1825–50, reproduced through the courtesy of the New York State Historical Association, Cooperstown.

In 1777, five years before the eagle became a part of the national seal, Congress adopted the flag of thirteen stars and thirteen stripes, and Americans delighted in having this waving symbol for their own land. Unfettered by official designs, they recreated it in a thousand variables and found a place for it, not only on flagstaffs, but on every conceivable object and on every possible occasion. The Stars and Stripes remain the basic element in our patriotic iconography.

One of the ever amazing aspects of the American Revolution and the formative years of the Republic is the large number of able and distinguished leaders that the scattered colonies were able to produce. Any number of them had the makings of great popular heroes, but all the others were, as time went by, overshadowed by George Washington. Except for the petulant sniping over the years of an occasional writer, the admiration for the first president has been almost universal. And it is, I think, with a sense of relief that we read in James Thomas Flex-

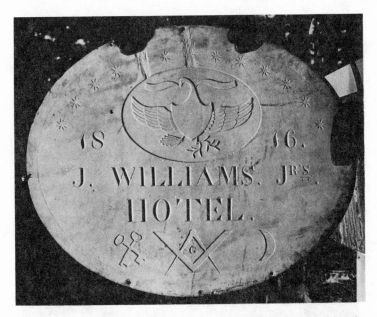

Williams Tavern Sign. Eagles frequently figure in tavern signs, but others of marble are unknown. John Williams' tavern in Ashfield, Massachusetts was, after 1826, the meeting place of the Masons. Anonymous, marble banded with iron, 30¼" x 38", c. 1826, reproduced through the courtesy of the New York State Historical Association, Cooperstown.

ner's exhaustive and most recent biography a reaffirmation of the facts that support our respect for the man who was, however trite it may sound, First in war, First in peace, and First in the hearts of his countrymen.

From the time the Revolution was over, Washington was The Great Man, and with his death in 1799 he came as close to being deified as we have ever come in this country. The flood of paintings, drawings, needlework that showed Americans in sorrow beside his tomb gave rise to a new art form in this country, the memorial in which death, the tomb, the willow reflected grief and honor to the departed. Forty years after Washington's death, Daniel Webster could say, at the dedication of

Liberty in the Form of the Goddess of Youth Giving Support to the Bald Eagle. This engraving was the source for scores of watercolor, needle-work, and oil paintings, including *Liberty and Washington*. The eagle, flag, liberty cap, the desecration of symbols of royalty are all included. Edward Savage, engraving, 23″ x 14¾″, 1796, reproduced through the courtesy of the New York State Historical Association, Cooperstown.

Liberty and Washington. Originally a tavern window shade, this naive painting retains Liberty, the eagle, liberty cap, the flag but adds the pine tree and Washington's bust, replacing the Order of the Garter with the Crown, but its indebtedness to Savage is unmistakable. Anonymous, oil on canvas, 6'2" x 3'8", c. 1800–1810, reproduced through the courtesy of the New York State Historical Association, Cooperstown.

the Bunker Hill monument, "I would cheerfully put the question today to the intelligence of Europe and the world, — what character of the century upon the whole stands out in the relief of history most pure, most respectable, most sublime, and I doubt not that by a suffrage approaching to unanimity, the answer would be Washington."

Not only did artists like the Peales, Stuart, and Trumbull paint Washington, but school girls in their classes, engravers and the painters of tavern signs and political banners, used Washington as the symbol of all that was best and noblest in American life. Not only was Washington himself a symbol of veneration, but Martha Washington came to epitomize wifely virtue and domestic tranquility. Mount Vernon became a national shrine very early. Artists portrayed Mount Vernon and the tomb on every conceivable object and on popular engravings that were copied over and over again. In 1850 the State of New York established Washington's Headquarters in Newburgh as the first historic site to be set aside by a governmental agency. Three years later the Mount Vernon Ladies' Association restored his property, and to this day it remains a temple of patriotic devotion.

My favorite synthesis of all of the elements of American iconography comes together in an anonymous painting on a window shade which once hung with eleven others like it in a Connecticut tavern. This is the famous *Liberty and Washington* which is based on Savage's *Liberty* but with its own special spirit. In its naive enthusiasm it shows us a youthful, classical Liberty with flag, pine tree, and liberty cap. The eagle flies overhead; while due honors are paid with a laurel wreath to the togaed bust of Washington, Liberty crushes the British Crown beneath her sandaled foot.

As years went by, no one replaced Washington, but other heroes moved in beside him. First of all, Andrew Jackson, who appears frequently in the drawings of school boys and girls and occasionally as a tavern sign. Around Henry Clay and his campaign for internal improvements there developed a body of symbols brought together in Neagle's portrait but repeated in such things as the political banner from Auburn, New York that we see in this collection: the plow, the canal, commerce, the

Andrew Jackson Sign. Probably a tavern sign, this polychromed iron silhouette is one of many material reminders of the intense popularity of Jackson. Anonymous, sheet iron polychromed on one side, 47" high, c. 1830, reproduced through the courtesy of the New York State Historical Association, Cooperstown.

cattle, the farm tools and implements, all these were symbols which his political campaigns utilized repeatedly. Certainly with a large majority of his countrymen, despite waves of criticism, Abraham Lincoln was a national hero long before the war was over. You don't hear songs like "We're Coming Father Abraham" for a man who is not a national hero. After the war the Lincoln myth and the Lincoln story became deeply embedded in our folklore. As with Washington, the stories were not necessarily true; people merely wanted to be able to believe

Mount Vernon Paddlebox Decoration. The steamboat *Mount Vernon* was built in 1846 and sailed out of Philadelphia. Everything about George Washington became an object of reverence. When boats passed his resting place at Mount Vernon the bell was tolled, and men bared their heads and stood at attention. Anonymous, wood, 25½" x 76", c. 1846, reproduced through the courtesy of the New York State Historical Association, Cooperstown.

them, for them to survive. Lincoln represented other sides of the American people than had Washington. He was poor where Washington was rich; he was of the prairie where Washington was of the tidewater. Until his presidency, he had moved with humble people, whereas Washington had moved with leaders; he had humor where Washington had dignity; there was a homely old shoe quality about him that found no counterpart in the Father of His Country. And yet they shared integrity and dedication and a profound concern for the people. Each faced terribly difficult times and provided a leadership for those times without which the country, in either instance, could not have survived. Many a leader in recent decades has hoped that he would form a triumvirate with those two, but no man has reached that eminence in the unanimous love and admiration of his fellow countrymen.

Mount Vernon became a symbol for Washington and for the Republic as have certain other places and buildings. Very early, in paintings and prints, we see Niagara Falls fulfilling that role, but the same has been true of the Capitol at Washington, Independence Hall, the White House, Washington's Mon-

Clay Political Banner. Originally the center of a square banner to be carried by Henry Clay's adherents in Auburn, New York, this is filled with the same symbols used by John Neagle in his portrait of Clay, widely known through engravings. Terence J. Kennedy, oil on canvas, 5'5" diameter, c. 1844.

ument, and in the last hundred years the Statue of Liberty in New York harbor. The Statue of Liberty is really far more a French conception of that lady than American, and yet we have taken her very much to our hearts.

Finally, there is one other American iconographic figure

Abraham Lincoln. Carved from a single log, this work was kept by the artist in his kitchen for company. Moran was a house carpenter and carver of decorative elements for interiors. Frank Moran, wood, c. 1940, reproduced through the courtesy of the New York State Historical Association, Cooperstown.

Justice of the Peace Sign. This wooden cut-out of Justice nourishing the eagle was placed over the gate of a justice of the peace in Appleton, Ohio. Anonymous, wood, polychromed on both sides, 22″ x 30″, c. 1880, reproduced through the courtesy of the New York State Historical Association, Cooperstown.

that we all recognize and while we see him with a smile we see in him also something of ourselves. The strange, ironic route by which the Troy meat wholesaler, Samuel Wilson, became Uncle Sam, the universally recognized symbol for the people and government of the United States, is far too long to be retold here. Fortunately, it has been happily covered in Alton Ketchum's *Uncle Sam: The Man and the Legend*. We see him in many forms and many places. I am always pleased when I see him standing in silhouette as a device for holding a country mailbox. Actually, he appears most frequently in the newspaper cartoons where he is apt to reflect the dilemmas with which we are faced or the mistakes that we have made.

Back of all these symbols is a great power of emotion that men and women felt for their country at every stage of its history: sometimes with hope, sometimes with despair, sometimes with deep concern. The arrogant young optimism of the 1820s and thirties and forties seems sadly out of place today. Yet some of the ebullience, some of the confidence in the future, some of the belief in ourselves can be a useful elixir in today's dark and threatened world.

THREE EYES ON THE PAST

was composed in 10-point Compugraphic Caledonia and leaded two points
by Metricomp Studios,
with display type in Deepdene by J. M. Bundscho, Inc.;
printed on 50-pound, acid-free Glatfelter Antique Cream,
adhesive-bound with Corvon 220-13 covers,
by Maple-Vail Book Manufacturing Group, Inc.;
and published by

SYRACUSE UNIVERSITY PRESS
SYRACUSE, NEW YORK 13210